A
NEW WAY
TO USE YOUR BEAN:

Developing Thinking Skills
in Children

Darlene Freeman

Trillium Press
New York

For my dedicated and enterprising parents, Mildred and Louis Freeman
who helped create the cook.

For my supportive and gifted sister and friend, Elaine Freeman -who instilled confidence in
the cook.

For my number one resource and inspiration, Cece Nadeau - who showed me the way to the
kitchen.

For my special friend and sounding board, Tom Kemnitz - who encouraged me to share the
recipes.

MANY THANKS TO:

Sandra N. Kaplan - for introducing me to the whole shebang.
Paula Strassman (wherever you are) - for sharing the beginning of many creative years to follow.
Avi Stachenfeld - for recognizing the heavy burden of a great potential.
Stanley Seidman - for allowing me to develop that great potential.
Jean Delp - for encouraging this non-dietetic approach to teaching thinking skills.
The children in my K-1 classes at Hunter College Elementary School (1978-79, 1979-80) for generating
an abundance of warmth, cooperation, humor, energy, creativity and intelligence.
Geoffrey Horlick - for creating a task-commitment model.
David Tucker - for helping to prove that even basketball champs can make it through medical
school.
Stuart Offner - for helping me to see how buildings are like bananas.
Ron Feinstein - for helping to make learning the laws of relativity more enticing than downing a hot
fudge sundae.

Copyright © 1982, Darlene Freeman. All Rights Reserved.
Trillium Press, Inc.
Box 921
Madison Square Station
New York, NY 10159
(212)-684-7399

ISBN: 0-89842-019-0
LC: 80-54766

TABLE OF CONTENTS

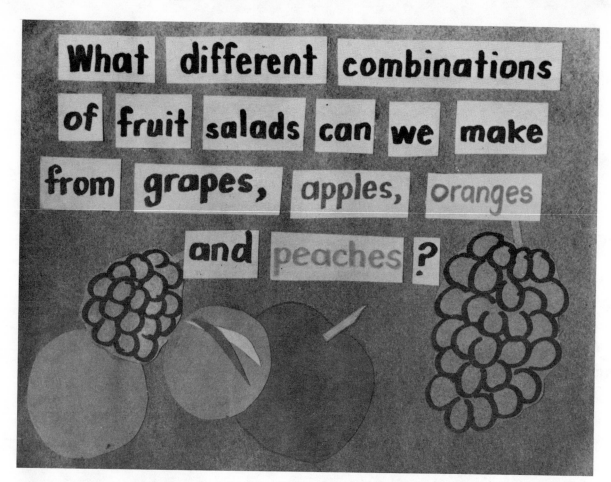

ill. 1

ill. 2

INTRODUCTION

A New Way to Use Your Bean is an outgrowth of several years of ongoing curricula development I have done at the Hunter College Elementary School in New York City - a school for intellectually gifted children. The book uses cooking to introduce youngsters to four thinking processes: critical thinking, creative thinking, logic, and problem solving. The cooking experiences serve as a generator for the development of this goal. Experiences with which the children will be involved will extend beyond the kitchen and will help youngsters recognize the fact that learning is not merely an accumulation of isolated facts and concepts. Instead, learning is viewed as a process that involves an accumulation and a creation of new ideas. Students will be given an opportunity to exercise and to strenghten their potential for understanding and organizing existing phenomena in their environment, as well as motivating them to create and to add new dimensions to it.

Thinking processes can be defined as a means of ordering the world an individual knows, giving insight into the unknown and strengthening one's ability to create. Specifically, critical thinking is the breaking down of the whole into its parts. It involves activities such as sorting, classifying, analyzing, comparing, and contrasting. Creative thinking involves helping children to become fluent and flexible thinkers which in turn will strengthen their abilities to create new and unusual solutions to problems, to create original products and to recognize new problems in a given situation. Brainstorming is involved, as well as developing the students' skills in combining elements that are the same or apparently different. Logic involves going from the general to the specific or from the specific to the general. It includes activities such as making inferences, using analogies, making predictions, seeing causes and effects and patterning. Problem solving involves defining a problem, analyzing information, hypothesizing, developing research skills, validating, and judging. It does not only include formal investigation. It can include solving problems that come up daily. Many of you have probably utilized some of these processes in units and activities you've developed with your class or with your own children.

It is clear that thinking processes cannot be developed independent of content area in prescribed curricula or in social situations. In addition, these processes cannot be taught as if they are mutually exclusive. They are threads that run through and connect all areas. In order to clarify this idea to students, the thinking processes developed in each cooking experience in this book are extended to other curricula areas, other areas of interest, and other experiences. Each different academic or social experience used to help teach thinking processes can be compared to members of a volleyball game, cooperating to hit the ball over the net. Each experience scores a point by helping the individual assimilate these skills into all areas of his/her life.

An ideal quality of cooking is that it is a relaxed way to challenge children and to develop their thinking skills. It requires little or no prior experience. Children, as young as pre-schoolers, associate cooking with pleasurable and other positive thoughts. Psychologically, a child experiences a sense of security working closely with someone in the kitchen. He/she also senses a feeling of satisfaction at the completion of a task which is relatively non-taxing when compared to assignments associated with academic subjects, such as analyzing the amendments to our constitution, or at a younger level, decoding words. Although the thinking processes used in cooking may be as sophisticated, similar or the same as those employed in a history, math or reading assignment, the content area is less threatening. Cooking's element of stresslessness encourages risk taking which is an essential ingredient in the creation and production of new and original ideas. It therefore would be a pleasurable way to begin or to reinforce higher level thinking processes.

1

A GUIDE FOR USING THE BOOK

EVALUATE YOUR CHILDREN'S THINKING SKILLS:
The chapters in this book have been arranged in order of increasing sophistication. It is not necessary to begin with the first chapter if the children with whom you work have aready mastered those skills. On the other hand, you might adjust any chapter to better suit the youngster's needs.

USE ACCURATE VOLCABULARY:
If you skim through the book you will notice that the directions for children include a number of technical terms such as "criteria," "evaluate," "predict," "diagram," "process," etc. Do not hesitate to explain and to use these words with the children. Youngsters generally love to learn new words. This is a good opportunity to develop their vocabulary and their communication skills.

ACQUAINT YOURSELF WITH EACH CHAPTER BEFORE PRESENTING THE EXPERIENCES TO THE CHILDREN:
Each chapter is divided into five sections: Thinking Processes Utilized, Materials and Equipment, Pre-Cooking Activities, Cooking Suggestions, and Post-Cooking Follow-Up. It is important to read each part carefully in order to make all necessary preparations and to become familiar with the thinking processes being developed so they can be extended to other areas of study and other realms of interest. I have tried to keep the amount of preparation to a minimum knowing how crucial the time element always is at home and at school.

DECIDE HOW YOU WOULD LIKE TO USE EACH CHAPTER:
This book can be used in a number of ways. With younger children an adult can organize, present and share each experience. On the other hand, older children can be guided to use this book by themselves or in small groups as part of an independent project. In addition, an adult might want to introduce a concept or activity to the entire group or to an individual child in order to clarify a question or a task before a youngster begins to work independently.

ORGANIZE THE SIZE OF THE COOKING GROUP TO MEET YOUR NEEDS:
The number of children who can cook at a particular time will depend upon the size of your kitchen or cooking area, the age and capabilities of the children, the number of supervising adults, and the amount of available utensils. The cooking experience might vary from lesson to lesson.

USE THE SUGGESTED EXPERIENCES AS A GUIDE:
The questions, activities, and recipes included in the book are guides for developing particular thinking skills. Feel free to add and/or substitute other questions, activities, and recipes to enhance each experience.

RECORD THE NEWLY DEVELOPED IDEAS:
Saving children's diagrams and pictures is a helpful device that can be used to reinforce skills that are introduced in each lesson. Children enjoy reexamining previous work and feel proud when they see their work compiled in a display product. Parents can combine the diagrams and pictures into one book. Teachers can make individual class books for each lesson. (See illustrations 1 and 2.)

INVOLVE THE CHILDREN WITH THE SAME THINKING PROCESSES IN MANY DIFFERENT WAYS:

The suggested pre-cooking activites should be done once or twice a week or during the course of a few weeks. The scheduling depends upon the attention span of the child or children and other programmed events. In between these lessons try to incorporate the particular skills and kinds of questions introduced and developed in each chapter in other experiences in which the child is involved. This will assist the child in recognizing the same thinking processes involved in different activities. In addition, it will help the child begin to see the relationships between apparently dissimilar experiences.

What are all the different ways you can use an apple?

1. <u>You can cook with apples.</u>   (Sarah)
apple pie, apple sauce, dried apples, apple pancakes, candied apples, apple juice...

2. <u>You can use apples to play games.</u>(Philip)
bobbing for apples, catch, apples on strings...

3. <u>You can use apples to plant apple trees.</u>(Ben)
Use the seeds.

4. <u>You can exercise by going apple picking.</u>
(Joseph)

5. <u>You can use apples for art projects.</u>(Kyla)
printing, sculpture...

6. <u>You can eat apples</u>. (Kristin)
An apple a day keeps the doctor away.

WHAT ARE ALL THE DIFFERENT WAYS YOU CAN USE AN APPLE?

THINKING PROCESSES UTILIZED

Creative Thinking:
-Regrouping in order to develop fluent, flexible and original thinking

Problem Solving:
-Collecting information to get a better understanding of a product

MATERIALS AND EQUIPMENT

Ingredients:
-apples (about one pound for every cup of applesauce)
-sugar
-cinnamon

Utensils:
-a strainer
-a corer

Other Preparation:
-a biography of Johnny Appleseed
-an experience chart for a class lesson (or a small piece of paper for an individual lesson)
-a duplicated diagram for each child (see ill. 4)

PRE-COOKING ACTIVITIES

ACTIVITY #1 *Read the biography of Johnny Appleseed to familiarize children with the history of the apple in the United States.*

-A good version of this biography is *Johnny Appleseed* by Eva Moore, Scholastic Press

ACTIVITY #2 *Arrange for a trip to an apple orchard.*

-How many different ways can you gather the apples?

What are the different ways you can use _____ ?

Use the other side if you have more ideas.

ill. 4

What are the different ways you can use _a key_ ?

DAViD age 6

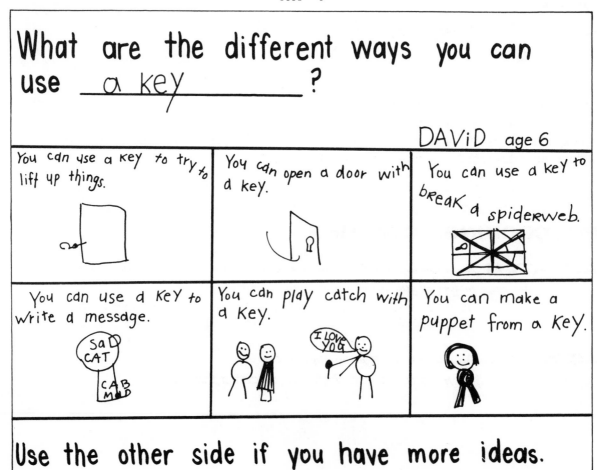

You can use a key to try to lift up things.	You can open a door with a key.	You can use a key to break a spiderweb.
You can use a key to write a message.	You can play catch with a key.	You can make a puppet from a key.

Use the other side if you have more ideas.

ill. 5

ACTIVITY #3 *What are all the different ways you can use an apple?*

-Record children's responses on an experience chart or small piece of paper depending on the size of the group (see ill. 3).

COOKING SUGGESTIONS

Here is a simple recipe for applesauce:

-Put the apples through a sectioned corer.
-Place the cored apple slices in a saucepan.
-Partly cover them with water.
-Simmer the apples until tender.
-Strain the apples.
-Add sugar and/or cinnamon to taste.

POST-COOKING ACTIVITIES

ACTIVITY #1 *Develop children's abilities to become fluent, flexible and original thinkers.*

-Distribute a copy of the diagram in illustration 4 to each child.
-Analyze the diagram with the children.
-Each child selects an object and creates as many different uses for that object as possible (see ill. 5).

ACTIVITY #2 *Develop brainstorming skills in other situations in which the child is involved.*

-What are all the different ways you can use an old egg carton?
-What different things in our environment can you think of that are transparent?
-What are all the different ways you can make a circle?
-What are all the different ways you can rename "ten"?
-What are all the different ways you can get to your grandmother's house?
-What are all the different ways you can describe yourself?
-What are all the different ways you can get a rhythm instrument to vibrate?
-What are all the different things you can do by yourself if everyone else is busy?
-What are all the different ways animal homes have influenced the construction of human homes (see ills. 6 & 7)?
-What are all the ways Bach's Fifth Brandenburg Concerto is different from Duke Ellington's Concerto for Cootie?

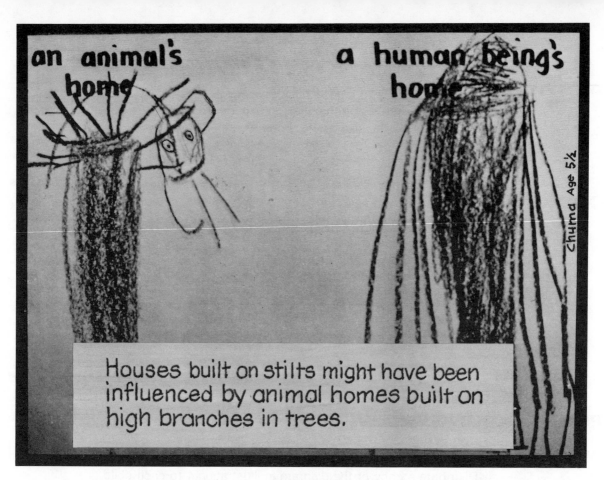

an animal's home

a human being's home

Chuma Age 5½

Houses built on stilts might have been influenced by animal homes built on high branches in trees.

ill. 6

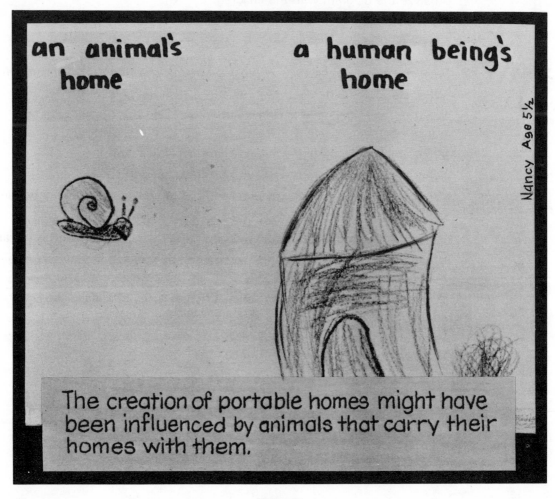

an animal's home

a human being's home

Nancy Age 5½

The creation of portable homes might have been influenced by animals that carry their homes with them.

ill. 7

HOW MANY DIFFERENT WAYS CAN YOU MAKE BUTTER?

THINKING PROCESSES UTILIZED

Critical Thinking:
-comparing different methods for doing the same task

Creative Thinking:
-redesigning methods to complete a task
-brainstorming to generate ideas

Logic:
-seeing cause and effect relationships

Problem Solving:
-defining problems
-doing research in order to collect information on different ways to prepare butter

MATERIALS AND EQUIPMENT

Ingredients:
-heavy cream
-salt (optional)

Utensils:
-bowl
-jar
-other utensils suggested by children

Other Preparation-
-drawing paper
-markers or crayons
-a diagram for each child (see ill. 8); the number of arrows included in the diagram can be
 increased

PRE-COOKING ACTIVITIES

ACTIVITY #1 *Find different ways to make butter.*

-How can we find different ways to make butter?

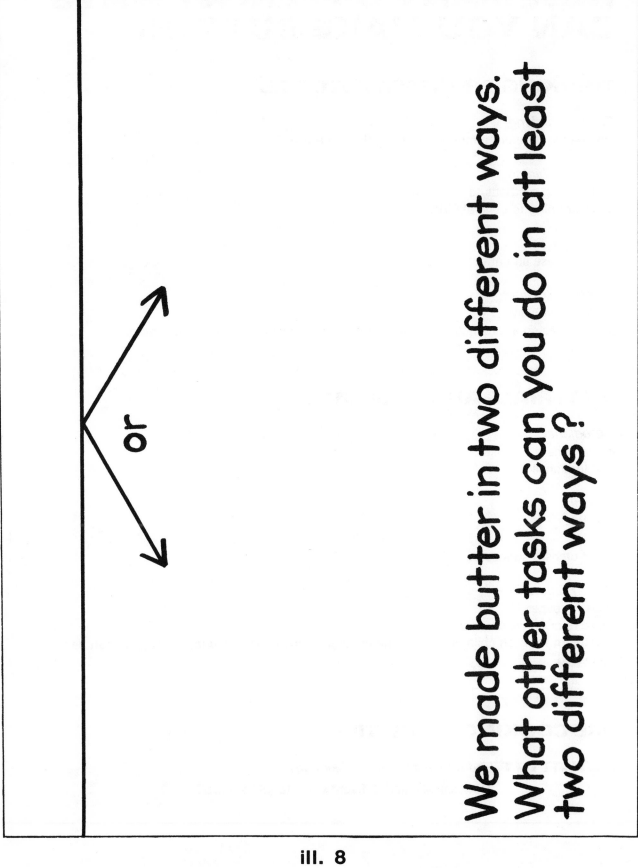

or

We made butter in two different ways. What other tasks can you do in at least two different ways?

ill. 8

ACTIVITY #2 *Collect information.*

-What are all the different ways we can make butter?

-List them.

-What are the ingredients and different utensils we will need in order to prepare butter in different ways? (For example, a jar for shaking the cream or an egg-beater for whipping the cream.)

-List them.

COOKING SUGGESTIONS

-Divide the class into small groups to prepare the butter in different ways.

-If the child is working at home, the task can be done in at least two different ways. Half the cream can be processed by the child. The other half of the cream can be processed in a different way by an adult, friend or sibling.

POST-COOKING ACTIVITIES

ACTIVITY #1 *Develop the concept that the same task can be done in a variety of ways.*

-Think of all the different kinds of tasks you can do in at least two different ways.

-Record your ideas in a diagram (see ills. 9 & 10).

ACTIVITY #2 *Design specific tasks for the children to complete in as many different ways as possible.*

-How many different ways can you color half the area of a square?

-Build a musical instrument.
 How many different ways can you make it vibrate?

-How many different ways can you get an ice-cube to melt?

-How many different endings can you create to finish a particular story?

-How many different ways can you help your younger sibling learn to read?

-How many different ways can you make a birdhouse?

ill. 9

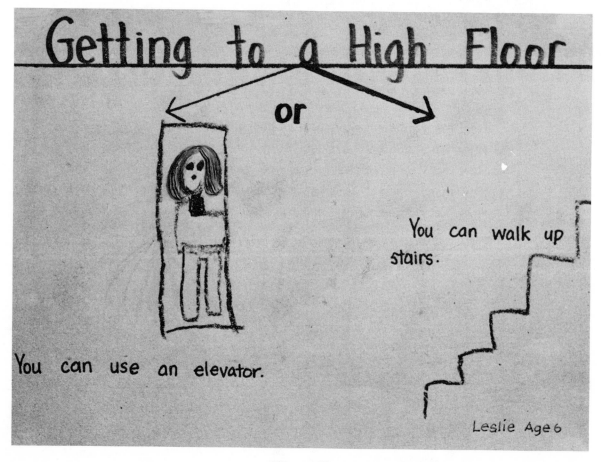

ill. 10

WHAT ARE ALL THE DIFFERENT PROCESSES YOU CAN PERFORM ON AN EGG?

THINKING PROCESSES UTILIZED

Critical Thinking:
-dissecting a problem to arrive at several different solutions

Creative Thinking:
-brainstorming to find different recipes for eggs

Logic:
-seeing cause and effect relationships of different processes applied to eggs

Problem Solving:
-defining problems
-collecting information to solve a problem
-recording and planning by graphing

MATERIALS AND EQUIPMENT

Ingredients and Utensils:
-This will depend upon the children's suggestions and research.

Other Preparation
-a chart-sized sheet of paper ruled into two inch squares to serve as a graph (see sample of completed graph in ill. 11).
-two inch paper squares - one for each person completing the graph
-experience chart paper or small sheet of paper, depending upon the size of the group

PRE-COOKING ACTIVITIES

ACTIVITY #1 *Define the problem.*

-We are going to have a brunch. We are going to serve eggs as the main course using as few extra ingredients as possible. We cannot use an oven or a frying pan. We can use a hot plate (or a regular range) and a regular pot.

-How many different ways can we prepare the eggs?

13

We're preparing a brunch. We're going to serve eggs. The only cooking implements available to us will be a hot plate and a small pot.

How do you plan to prepare your egg?

oliver				C HUMA				RH
NoAH				Nancy				
Kyoko								
Sheri				Cozzy				Sage
Thomas								
BO		AniKa		IsAAc		stePhen		L.L
boil		boil and slice		boil and devil		boil chop combine		poach

ill. 11

ACTIVITY #2 *Collect information.*

-How can we find more recipes for preparing eggs other than the ones you suggested?

-Collect and share as many different egg recipes as you can. Keep in mind the kinds of equipment that are available for our use.

ACTIVITY #3 *Plan the cooking experience.*

-Decide which of the shared egg recipes you would like to prepare.

-Record a picture of it on one of the small squared pieces of paper and glue it to the graph. (In preparing the skeleton of the graph, label each column with the different processes required to prepare each different egg recipe.)

ACTIVITY #4 *Analyze the graph.*

-Compare the number of children planning to prepare each recipe.

-Based on the completed graph, list the ingredients, the amount of ingredients, and the utensils the children will need in order to prepare the egg. (Record the children's responses.)

COOKING SUGGESTIONS

An excellent book to use with this lesson is: *What to Do with an Egg,* by Francoise Blanchet and Rinke Doornekamp (Barron's Educational Series, Inc., 113 Crossways Park Drive, Woodbury, New York 11797).

POST-COOKING ACTIVITIES

ACTIVITY #1 *Find solutions to other problems.*
(This will depend upon the child's interests and areas of study.)

-Design a musical instrument which makes at least three different sounds.

-Design a playroom with an area of 20 square units.
The room can be any shape.
It should include areas for breakable items, quiet activities, and other special needs.
Justify the shape you design for your playroom.

-If you had only a dollar bill, and you needed the exact fare of 60 cents to get on a bus, what are all the different ways you could try to get change?

-If you wanted to plant a seed, but you were unable to use soil, what other ways could you get the seed to grow?

-The following two children's series contain stories that develop the skill of finding solutions to problems:

Encyclopedia Brown - Donald Sobol
Basil the Mouse - Eve Titus

HOW MANY DIFFERENT WAYS CAN YOU DECORATE A CUPCAKE?

THINKING PROCESSES UTILIZED

Critical Thinking:
-analyzing a problem to arrive at a solution

Creative Thinking:
-generating new ideas by restating old ones

Logic:
-predicting the effects of various processes

Problem Solving:
-defining problems

MATERIALS AND EQUIPMENT

Ingredients:
-flour
-liquid shortening
-sugar
-eggs
-milk

Utensils:
-mixing bowls
-large spoons
-measuring spoons
-muffin tin

Other Preparation:
-chart paper or small sheet of paper depending on the size of the group
-blank copies of the diagram in illustration 12
-copies of the diagram in illustration 13

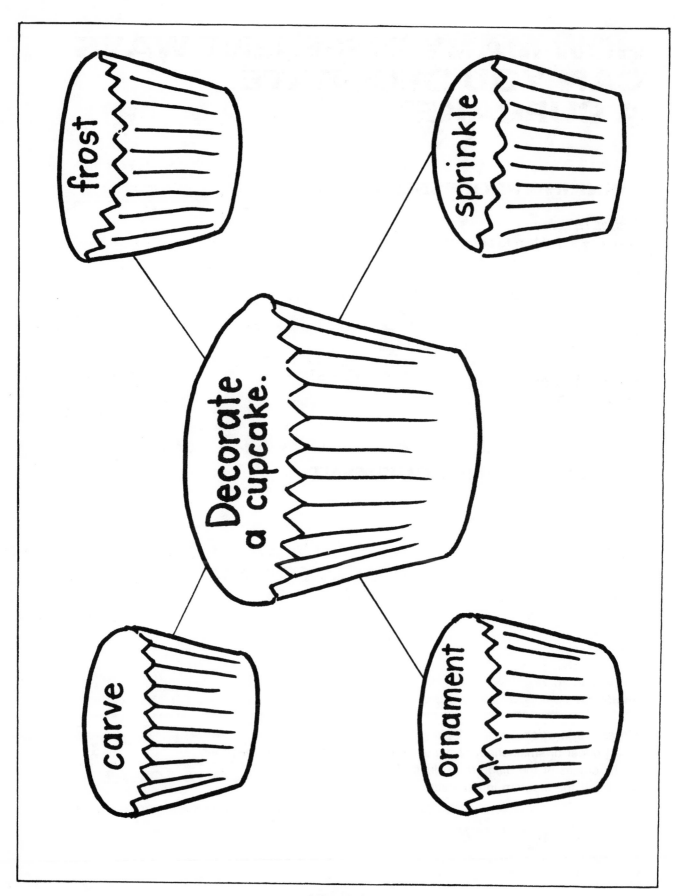

frost

sprinkle

Decorate a cupcake.

carve

ornament

ill. 12

PRE-COOKING ACTIVITIES

ACTIVITY #1 *Define problems.*

-List the problems you would have to consider before decorating your cupcake.

-Record the children's responses.

ACTIVITY #2 *Think about different ways of decorating a cupcake.*

-Do a sample plan with the children by listing all the different processes you can use to decorate a cupcake.

-Record the children's responses on a large diagram (see ill. 12).

-Distribute individual blank diagrams for the children to create their own decorating plans.

COOKING SUGGESTIONS

Here is a simple recipe for making cupcakes which serves six:

YOU WILL NEED:
1 cup of flour
½ C of liquid shortening
½ C of sugar
1 egg
1 T of milk

PREHEAT the oven to 350 degrees.
GREASE the muffin tin.
COMBINE the flour and the shortening.
MIX the two ingredients.
STIR IN the sugar, the egg and the milk.
SPOON the mixture into the greased muffin tin.
BAKE in the oven until the mixture becomes golden brown.

POST-COOKING SUGGESTIONS

ACTIVITY #1 *Extend the idea of recognizing variations of the same process in other situations.*

-Examine the diagram in illustration 13.

-What different ways can you accomplish each different process (see ill. 14)?

-Think of a process that is not included in this diagram.

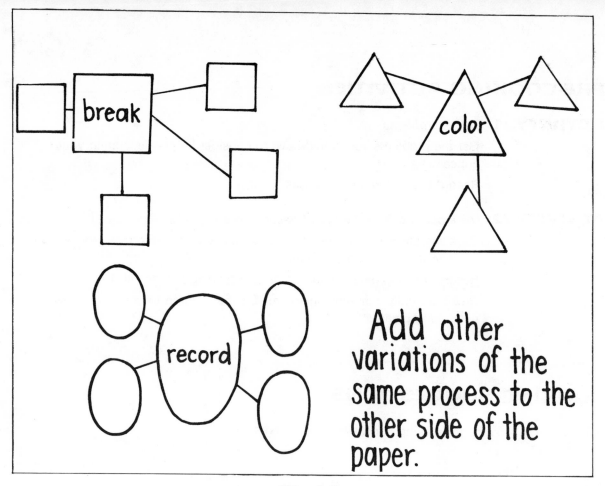

Add other variations of the same process to the other side of the paper.

ill. 13

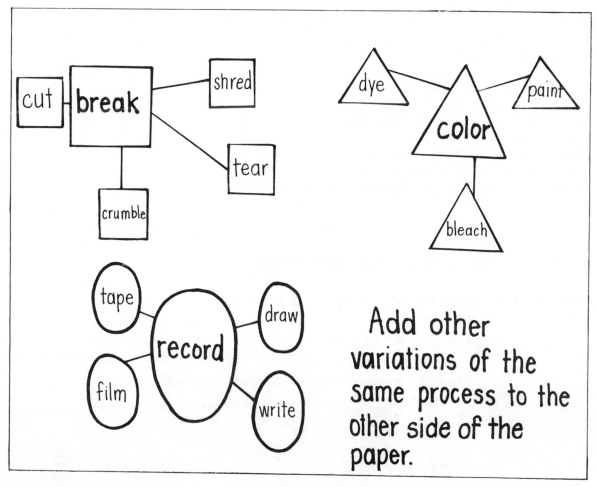

Add other variations of the same process to the other side of the paper.

ill. 14

Add it to the other side of the diagram and complete it in the same way as you completed the examples.

-Share your ideas with others (see ills. 15 & 16).

ACTIVITY #2 *Apply the idea of recognizing variations of the same process to practical situations.*

(This will depend upon the child's interests and on what he/she is studying. The following ideas are suggestions. You can continue to use the same kind of diagram as you did in ACTIVITY #1.)

-If you are planning to do an independent study, what are all the processes you can use to record your information (tape? film? draw?...)?

-If you are planning to go from California to New York, what different processes can you use for transportation (fly? drive? cycle?...)?

-If you were going to divide a piece of paper in half, what different processes could you use (cut? tear? rip?...)?

-What are the different processes pioneers used to gather food (trap? hunt? fish? grow?...)?

-What are the different processes you can use to exhibit one of your collections (hang? photograph? arrange? sort?...)?

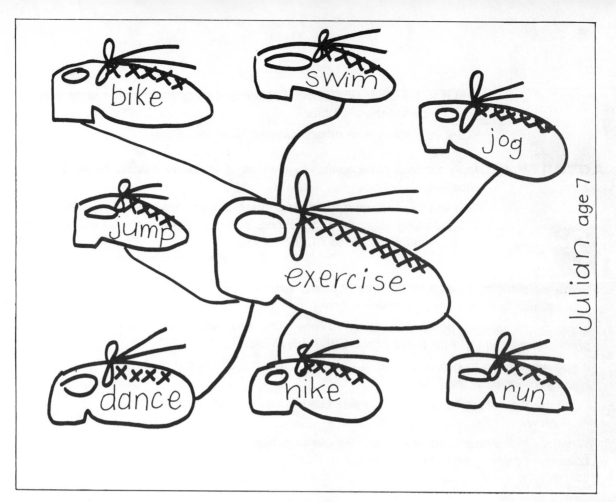

ill. 15

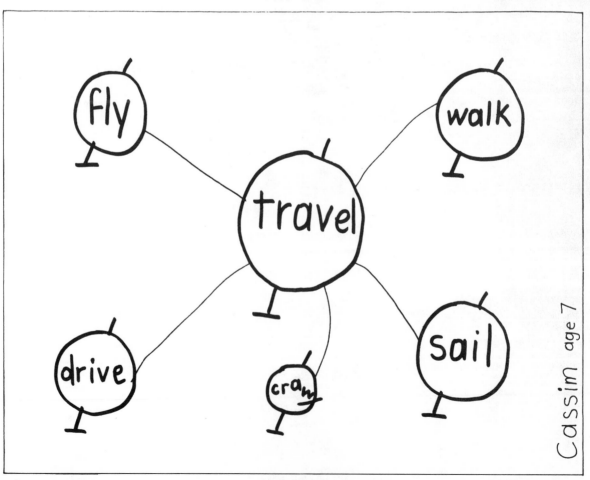

ill. 16

WHEN PREPARING A MACARONI SALAD, IS IT A GOOD IDEA TO ADD THE MAYONNAISE BEFORE YOU COOK THE MACARONI?

THINKING PROCESSES UTILIZED

Critical Thinking:
-ordering the cooking processes in order to organize the experience and to arrive at the best result
-analyzing the possibilities of ordering combinations

Creative Thinking:
-rearranging the sequence of processes in order to see the effect the arrangement has on a final product

Logic:
-making predictions about the final product based on the order in which it is prepared
-recognizing the effect order has in preparing a recipe and in other situations

Problem Solving:
-defining problems in order to organize the preparation of the macaroni salad
-validating the effects of order on the final product

MATERIALS AND EQUIPMENT

Ingredients:
-macaroni
-mayonnaise
-salt
-pepper
-water
-other ingredients suggested by children

Utensils:
-a stove or hot plate

Rearrange the cards in many different ways. Discover the effects of changing the sequence.

-a pot
-a mixing bowl
-a mixing spoon
-a measuring cup

Other Preparation:
-a list of ingredients for the macaroni salad (see Cooking Suggestions)
-an experience chart - or a small sheet of paper if you are working with an individual child
-sequence cards for a macaroni salad recipe
-sequence cards to represent other events (See ill. 17 for suggestions.)
-drawing paper
-crayons or magic markers

PRE-COOKING ACTIVITIES

ACTIVITY #1 *Analyze the ingredients and processes in the macaroni salad recipe.*

-What does each ingredient do for the macaroni salad? For example, the mayonnaise helps to add flavor and to keep the macaroni moist. The pepper adds spice.

-Can we combine each of the four ingredients in a bowl and automatically get macaroni salad?

ACTIVITY #2 *Recognize the importance of the order of the processes performed on each of the ingredients.*

-Prepare sequence cards that illustrate the preparation of a macaroni salad.

-Arrange the sequence cards in the order we plan to prepare the macaroni salad.

-Rearrange the cards.
 Explain the effects of rearranging the processes.

ACTIVITY #3 *Improve the macaroni salad.*

-List the ingredients and processes we might add to the macaroni salad to improve it.

-Select some of the children's suggestions to use as part of the cooking experience.

COOKING SUGGESTIONS

Here is a simple macaroni salad recipe which serves approximately five:

   BOIL enough water to cover 2 cups of macaroni.

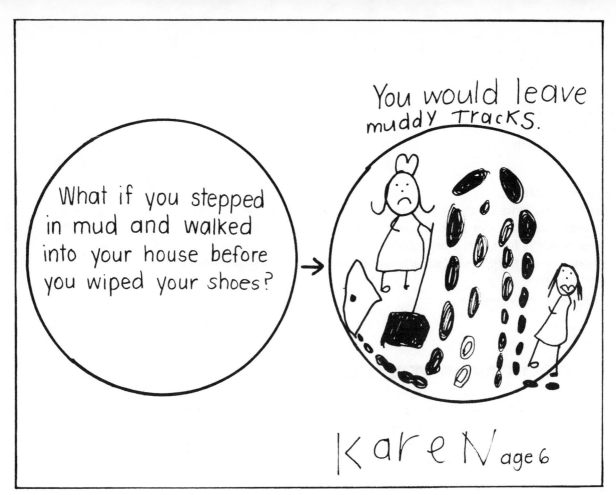

ill. 18

ill. 19

ADD 2 cups of macaroni to the boiling water.
COOK the macaroni until it starts to soften.
POUR out the water.
ADD ½ a cup of mayonnaise to the macaroni.
ADD salt and pepper to taste.
ADD children's suggestions.
STIR and SERVE.

POST-COOKING ACTIVITIES

ACTIVITY #1 *Reinforce the importance of sequencing.*

-Use sequence card games to develop this skill. (See ill. 17 for sample.)

-Rearrange the cards to see the various effects of changing the sequence of events.

-Can you think of a series of events in which the order would not affect the final product?

ACTIVITY #2 *Extend the idea of sequencing to other areas.*

-Why are the words in a dictionary arranged in alphabetical order?

-Why can't you learn how to read before you learn how to speak?

-What whole numbers precede ten?
 What helped you to remember them?

-What importance does order play in your name?
 What importance does order play in your telephone number?

-In what other areas of your life does order have importance?

ACTIVITY #3 *Change the order of events to see the effects on the final outcome.*

(These ideas can be illustrated in drawings. See sample drawings in ills. 18, 19, 20, & 21.)

-What if you squeezed an uncapped tube of toothpaste before you took out your toothbrush?

-What if you put on your shoes before you put on your socks?

-What if you got on your bicycle before you put air into the tires?

-What if you emptied some of your money from your piggy bank before knowing what you were going to buy?

-What if you wanted to read before you went to sleep, but turned off the light before you got into bed?

-Think of other mixed-up events to illustrate.

ill. 20

ill. 21

HOW CAN YOU CREATE A PATTERNED SNACK FROM CREAM CHEESE AND/OR JELLY AND MATZO?

THINKING PROCESSES UTILIZED

Critical Thinking:
-comparing and contrasting in order to arrive at a definition for "pattern"
-dissecting the ingredients in order to become more familiar with their attributes

Creative Thinking:
-rearranging the ingredients to create the most desirable pattern
-substituting one ingredient for another

Logic:
-patterning to help children make inferences and deductions
-transference of patterning concepts from cooking to other experiences

Problem Solving:
-hypothesizing about whether or not the pattern will work, particularly when a three-dimensional
 pattern is involved

MATERIALS AND EQUIPMENT

Ingredients:
-matzos or any other large crackers or pieces of bread
-cream cheese
-jelly

Utensils:
-knives
-spoons
-any utensils for creating patterns in the cream cheese
-plates or paper towels

Other Preparation:
-experience chart paper for an entire class lesson (or a small piece of paper for an individual
 experience)

How can you create a patterned snack from cream cheese and/or jelly and matzo?

1. You can alternate layers of cream cheese and matzo.
You can alternate layers of cream cheese, jelly and matzo. (Sascha)

2. You can make stripes on the matzo with jelly and/or cream cheese. (Alex).

3. You can spread cream cheese or jelly on a sheet of matzo.
Then you can create a pattern using crumbled matzo. (Titli.)

4. You can build a patterned structure. (Caroline)

5. You can use a utensil to make patterned lines. (Anne)

ill. 22

-drawing paper for each child
-crayons, markers or pencils

PRE-COOKING ACTIVITIES

ACTIVITY #1 *Define the idea of a pattern.*

-Direct the children's attention to three different children with three different patterned shirts.
How are the shirts the same?
How are the shirts different?

-Direct the children's attention to three different children with three different solid colored shirts.
How are those three children's shirts the same? How are they different?

-Compare the set of three patterned shirts to the set of three solid colored shirts.

-Establish a definition for a pattern.

-What are all the different patterns in our classroom?

ACTIVITY #2 *Dissect the ingredients.*
Substitute ingredients to suit individual tastes.

-Describe the qualities of cream cheese.

-Describe the qualities of jelly.

-Describe the qualities of matzo.

-If you don't like one of the ingredients, think of others you could substitute for it.

-What would you have to think about before you could make the substitution?

ACTIVITY #3 *Create the pattern.*

-How can you create a patterned snack from cream cheese, jelly and/or matzo?
Record the children's responses on an experience chart or small paper (see ill. 22).

COOKING SUGGESTIONS:

Keep the experience chart with the children's suggested patterns near the cooking table for those children who need help getting started and to refresh the other children's memories.

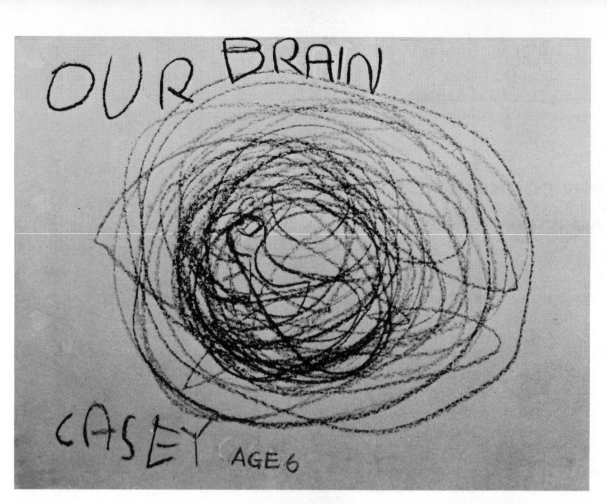

ill. 23

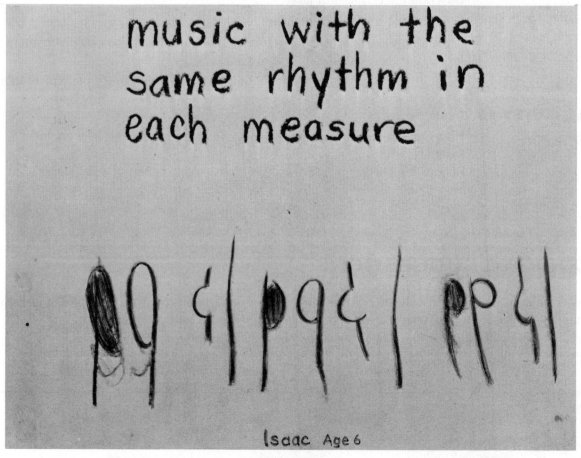

ill. 24

POST-COOKING ACTIVITIES:

ACTIVITY #1 *Record your snack.*

       -Describe your pattern.

       -Draw a picture of your snack.

       -Carefully record the pattern.

ACTIVITY #2 *Identify patterns in our environment.*

       -Draw, take photographs, or use magazine pictures to show things in our environment that have patterns (see ills. 23 & 24).

ACTIVITY #3 *Recognize patterns in specific curricular areas.*
The following are a few examples:

-Complete these patterns with at least two words that can follow:
       bat, cat, sat, —
       I'll, he'll, she'll —
       same, time, cane,—
       enormous, huge, tremendous, —

-Create your own word patterns.

-How many different patterns can you find in this series of numbers?

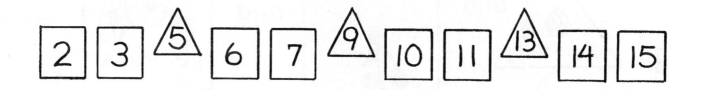

-Create number patterns for your friend to guess.

-Place plants in a sunny window.
Watch them grow.
List the patterns you observe.

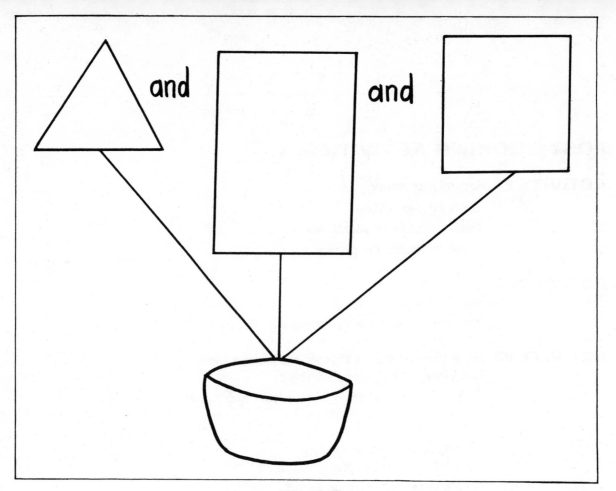

ill. 25

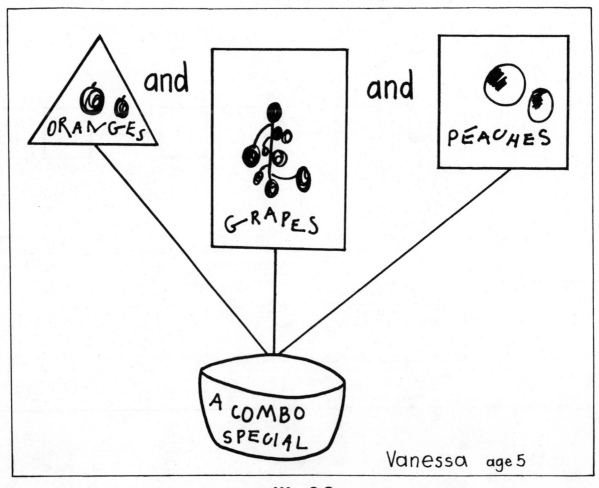

ill. 26

WHAT DIFFERENT COMBINATIONS OF FRUIT SALADS CAN WE MAKE FROM GRAPES, APPLES, ORANGES AND PEACHES?

THINKING PROCESSES UTILIZED

Critical Thinking:
-analyzing data to solve a problem

Creative Thinking:
-combining elements to create something new
-regrouping to see various combinations
-adding on to improve the original product

Logic:
-making deductions in order to name a recipe

Problem Solving:
-recording in order to collect and evaluate information
-judging in order to evaluate the effect of additional ingredients on the final product

MATERIALS AND EQUIPMENT

Ingredients:
-grapes
-apples
-oranges
-peaches
-or other fruits in season

Utensils
-cutting boards
-knives
-apple corers
-bowls
-spoons

What different combinations of fruit salads can we make from grapes, apples, oranges and peaches?

Most of the children used apples, oranges and grapes.

		O ᵇ O Grapes apples oranGes Kyla				
		O ᵇ O philip				
		ᵇ ☺ Raymond				
		ᵇ ᵇ ᵇᵇ DAViD		ᴼ ᴼ. Ben		
ᴼ O Anne		oranges ᴼᴼ.ᴼ ᴼᴼᴼ: KristiN		ᵇ ᵈ ᵇ ZacHarY		
O ᵍ 8 Vanessa		ᵈ O ◦ ALIsa		◎ O ᵈ Omar		ᵍ ◯ Titli
grapes oranges peaches		apples oranges grapes		apples oranges peaches		grapes apples peaches

ill. 27

Other Preparation:
-copies of two diagrams for each child (see ills. 25 & 28)
-a chart-size piece of graph paper with two inch squares, stating the following question at the top: What different combinations of fruit salads can we make from grapes, apples, oranges and peaches (see sample of completed graph in ill. 27)?
-two inch squared papers to accompany graph

PRE-COOKING ACTIVITIES

ACTIVITY #1 *Examine the fruits.*

Define the problem.

Make a plan.

-You can use three of the four fruits to prepare your own fruit salad.

-Name the three you would like to use.

-Take turns eliciting responses from the members of the group so that the children may recognize the variety of possible combinations.

ACTIVITY #2 *Record the various suggested fruit salad combinations on a large class or small group graph so the idea is visually represented.*

-Draw a picture on a two inch squared paper to record each of the three fruits you plan to use in the salad.

-Paste your picture on the appropriate part of the graph (see ill. 27).

ACTIVITY #3 *Evaluate the information on the graph.*

-How many children used "x" combination?
How many children used "y" combination? etc.

-Compare the numbers.
Does the graph represent all possible combinations of fruit salads we can make with those four fruits?

-List all the combinations you can think of that we did not include.

COOKING SUGGESTIONS

-A small group of children can cut all the fruit. The others can use the pre-cut fruit to prepare their individual salads.

-Each child can prepare his/her own salad from beginning to end.

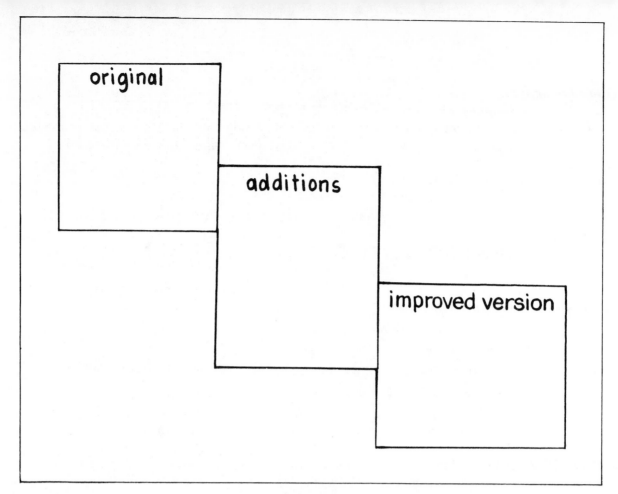

ill. 28

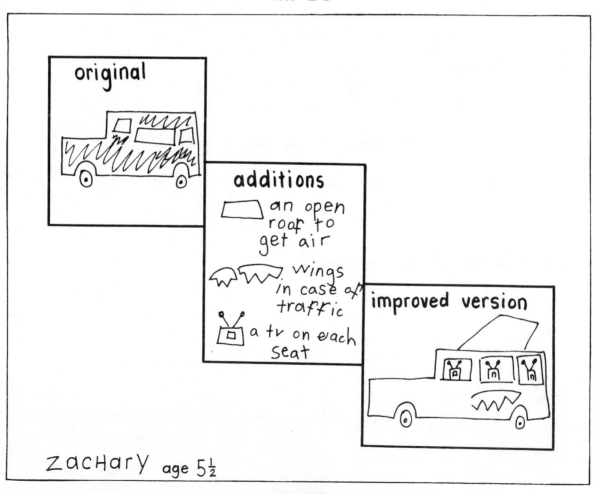

ill. 29

POST-COOKING ACTIVITIES

ACTIVITY #1 *Record individual recipes.*

-What are the purposes of recording individual fruit salad recipes in a book?

-Examine the diagram in illustration 25.

-How can we record our individual recipes using this diagram? (Older childre can design their own diagrams.)

ACTIVITY #2 *Name your recipe.*

-What information would be necessary to consider before naming your salac

-Add the name to your diagram (see ill. 26).

ACTIVITY #3 *Improve your salad.*

-What would you add to your original fruit salad to improve its appearance (taste?

-How would each of the ingredients you suggested improve the appearance or taste of your original salad?

ACTIVITY #4 *Improve something in your environment.*

-Choose something in your environment that you think needs improvement.

-Add as many different details in order to improve it.

-Record your ideas on the diagram (see ill. 29).

-Share your completed diagram with a friend.

-Does your friend have any additional ideas?

The Delicious
Apple TREAT
by NOAH age 6
=
An Apple.
+
Honey.
+
Coconut.
+
Peanuts.

CAN YOU COMBINE DIFFERENT INGREDIENTS TO CREATE YOUR OWN SNACK?

THINKING PROCESSES UTILIZED

Critical Thinking:
-analyzing the taste and quality of each ingredient to create a recipe
-ordering the ingredients to create the snack

Creative Thinking:
-combining to create something new

Logic:
-recognizing the effects of adding or combining various ingredients
-making analogies to create a descriptive name for the snack

Problem Solving:
-recording information in order to duplicate the recipe

MATERIALS AND EQUIPMENT

Ingredients:
-apples
-pears
-walnuts
-honey
-peanuts
-coconut
-cinnamon

Utensils:
-toothpicks
-knives
-spoons
-plates

Other Preparation:
-drawing paper
-pencils

THE GreaTESt TrEaT EVEr

bY RaJESH age 6½

$$\text{(sock)} = \text{pear} + \text{Honey} + \underset{\text{PEANuTS}}{OOO^O} + \underset{\substack{\text{cinn}\\\text{dmon}}}{ccccc}$$

ill. 31

A La Apple Cinnamon and Walnut

by oliver age 5½

Apple | Honey | Cinnamon | walnuts

ill. 32

PRE-COOKING ACTIVITIES

ACTIVITY #1 *Plan the snack.*

    -Examine the list of ingredients.

    -How can you combine some of the ingredients to create a snack?

COOKING SUGGESTIONS

-The ingredients listed under MATERIALS AND EQUIPMENT can be substituted.

-You can also add to the list.

POST-COOKING ACTIVITIES

ACTIVITY #1 *Create a name for the snack.*

    -Carefully look at your snack.

    -Think about all the different things it reminds you of.

    -Taste your snack.

    -What are good names for your snack?

ACTIVITY #2 *Record the snack.*

    -Prepare a diagram to show the ingredients you used in your snack.

    -Use plus signs (+).

    -See samples of completed diagrams in ills. 30, 31 & 32.

ACTIVITY #3 *Extend the idea of combining to create something new to other situations.*

    -What combination of equipment do you need to build a model airplane?

    -Combine various clues in a mystery to arrive at a solution.

    -What words can you combine to make compound words?

    -What elements do you have to combine to cause a melting chemical reaction?

    -What activities do you have to combine to create an exciting birthday party?

    -What ingredients do you have to combine to make a bubble bath?

    -What tinkertoy pieces do you have to combine to make a model of a ferris wheel?

    -What different sets can you combine to make the number ten?

What gourds can we include in our salad?

ill. 33

What beans can we include in our salad?

ill. 34

CAN YOU CLASSIFY THE INGREDIENTS OF YOUR SALAD?

THINKING PROCESSES UTILIZED

Critical Thinking:
-classifying ingredients in order to analyze them and to solve problems

Creative Thinking:
-regrouping ingredients to create something new
-combining different ingredients and processes to create something new

Logic:
-making deductions and inferences based on classification systems

Problem Solving:
-defining different processes to apply to each ingredient

MATERIALS AND EQUIPMENT

Ingredients and Utensils:
-These will depend upon the children's suggestions.

Other Preparation:
-Diagrams which can be included in an activity center, done with an entire class or completed individually (See ills. 33 & 34 for suggestions.)

PRE-COOKING ACTIVITIES

ACTIVITY #1 *Classify vegetables to include in a salad.*

-Name different gourds we can include in a salad.

-Name different beans we can include in a salad.

-Name different kinds of cabbages we can include in a salad.

-Use a diagram to record children's responses (see ills. 33 & 34).

-What other categories of vegetables can we include in a salad?

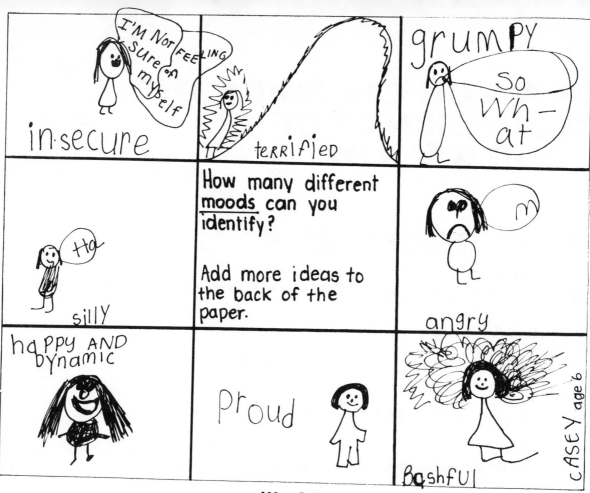

ill. 35

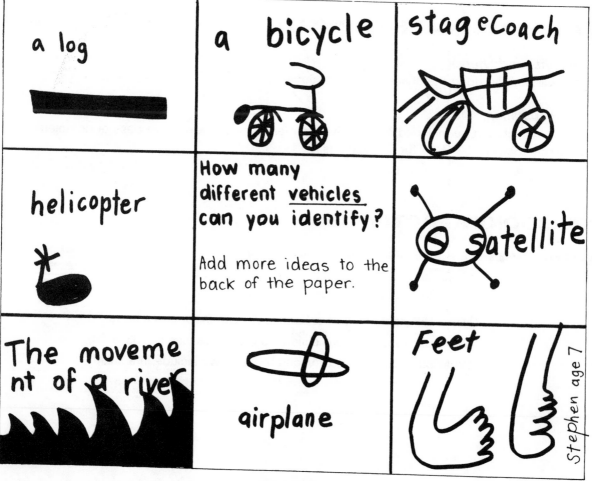

ill. 36

ACTIVITY #2 *Plan the salad.*

-List the gourds, cabbages, beans, etc., that you would like to include in a salad.

-Select different processes to apply to each of the vegetables.

-Record a plan. (See suggested diagrams in ills. 33 & 34.)

COOKING SUGGESTIONS

-Encourage children to create unusual versions of basic cooking processes, such as cutting a cucumber in many different ways or tearing leafy vegetables to form a pattern.

-Add your favorite salad dressing to the vegetables.

POST-COOKING ACTIVITIES

ACTIVITY #1 *Classify other ideas or objects.*

-Select a category.

-How many different facts, objects, or ideas can you list for each category?

-Record your responses. (See ills. 35 & 36 for sample responses.)

ACTIVITY #2 *Extend the idea of classification to daily situations.*

-If you are riding in a car and would like to put on a puppet show, but you left your puppets at home, what other objects could you use for puppets?

-Visit an art museum.
 Collect picture postcards of various styles of art.
 Sort the cards.
 Create your own style of art.
 Design different pieces of artwork that can be classified in that style.

-Help an adult sort the clean laundry.
 Put the sorted clothes in their appropriate places.

-Sort different kinds of fabrics in different ways.
 Which fabrics would make good rugs?
 Which fabrics would make good sheets?
 Give reasons to support your suggestions.

-Examine different kinds of plants.
 How are they the same?
 How are they different?
 Classify them according to their attributes.
 Hypothesize about why certain plants have the attributes they do.
 Read more about plants to see if you were right.

47

-Learn to count by 1's, by 5's, and by 10's.
 Why is it useful to know how to count by groups of numbers?

-How many different ways can you categorize your independent study topic so that you can find more information under different headings?

-In order to create a vivid picture for the reader what kinds of words can you use in a story you plan to write?

How would opposite processes affect the same object or situation?

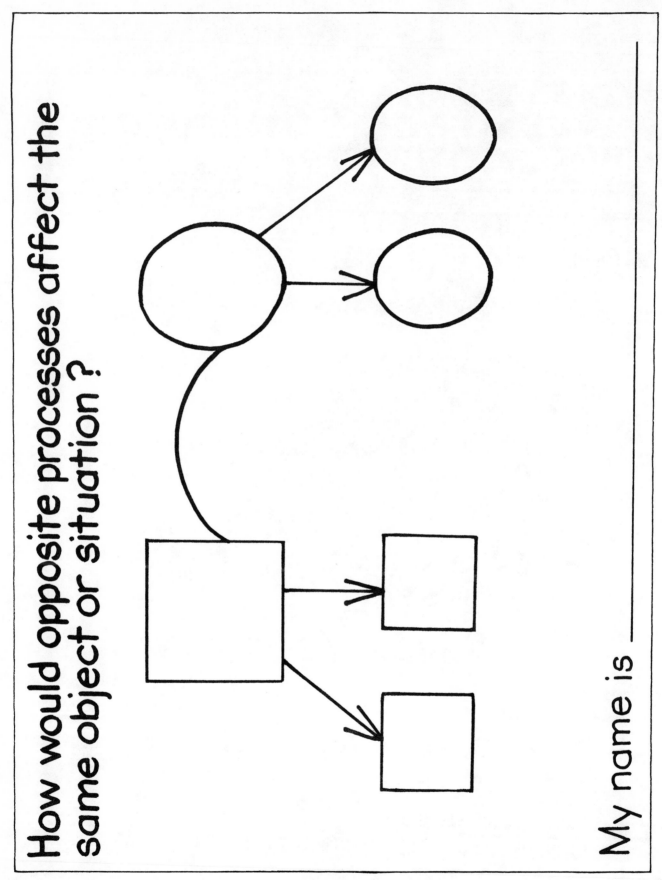

My name is _____

ill. 37

IF YOU ARE PREPARING TWO DESSERTS AND ONE IS GOING TO BE A TART LEMON PUDDING, WHAT OTHER KIND OF DESSERT CAN YOU PREPARE AS A CONTRAST TO THE LEMON PUDDING?

THINKING PROCESSES UTILIZED

Critical Thinking:
-classifying attributes to organize the problem
-making comparisons to gain a better understanding of the issues involved in solving a particular
 problem

Creative Thinking:
-reversing an idea to create something new

Logic:
-making analogies to personalize a problem
-recognizing cause and effect relationships after analyzing contrasting situations
-making predictions

Problem Solving:
-defining problems

MATERIALS AND EQUIPMENT

Ingredients and Utensils:
This will depend upon the children's suggestions or the adult's decisions (see COOKING
SUGGESTIONS).

Other Preparation:
-chart paper or a small sheet of paper, depending upon the size of the group
-a duplicated diagram for each child (see ill. 37)

Draw symbols that represent opposites.

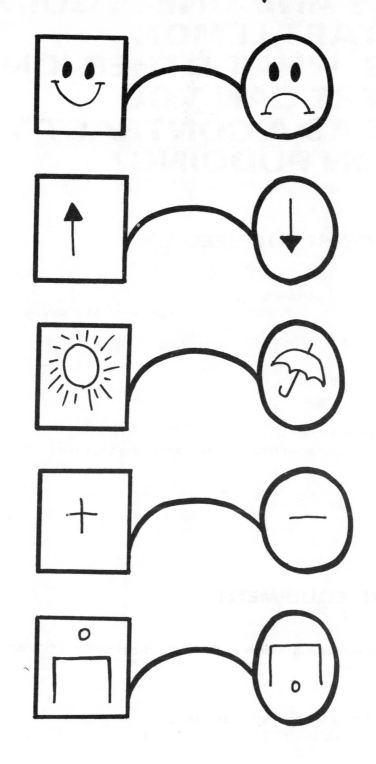

PRE-COOKING ACTIVITIES

ACTIVITY #1 *Define the problem.*

-What are the attributes of a lemon pudding?

-List other desserts that have the same attributes.

-What increases the tartness of a dessert?

-Record the children's responses.

ACTIVITY #2 *Use analogies to create a contrasting dessert.*

-List the attributes that would accompany a contrasting dessert to the lemon pudding.

-Use the list of contrasting attributes supplied by the children to prepare an analogy exercise.
Record the children's responses.
For example: a dessert as crunchy as...
a dessert as sweet as...
a dessert as chewy as...

ACTIVITY #3 *Analyze the responses to the analogy in order to arrive at a contrasting dessert.*

-What desserts match the descriptions of the analogies recorded in ACTIVITY #2?

-What ingredients suggested in the analogies would you combine to create a contrasting dessert to the lemon pudding?

COOKING SUGGESTIONS

-If necessary, begin this lesson by preparing a tart lemon pudding to allow children to experience the tartness before proceeding with PRE-COOKING ACTIVITY #1.

-Decide whether you would like the children to create their own dessert(s) or to follow a pre-written recipe that satisfies the problem.

POST-COOKING ACTIVITIES

ACTIVITY #1 *Extend the idea of contrast.*

-Draw symbols to represent opposite qualities in other phenomena in your environment. (See sample responses in ill. 38.)

-Think about how each set of opposites would affect the same object or situation in a different way. (See sample responses in ills. 39 & 40.)

How would opposite processes affect the same object or situation?

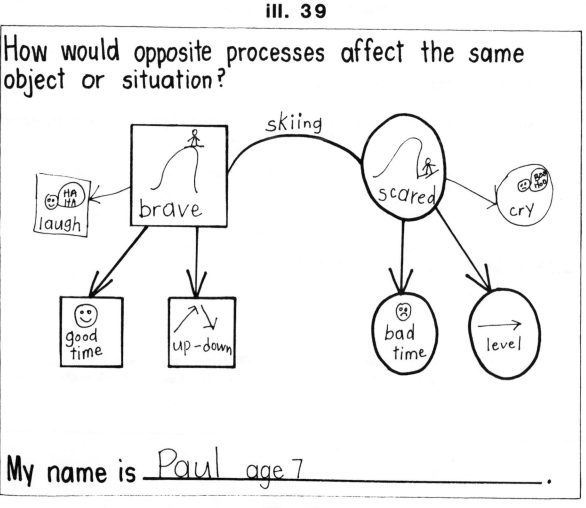

My name is __Mary__ age 6 .

ill. 39

How would opposite processes affect the same object or situation?

My name is __Paul__ age 7 .

ill. 40

ACTIVITY #2 *Use the idea of contrasting in order to solve problems.*

(Develop the activities around the children's interests and areas of study.)

-If you have mixed a color and it is too dark, what can you do to make it lighter?

-If you are at the top of the monkey bars and you are feeling scared, what opposite act can you perform to solve the problem?

-If a plant is sitting in a dark part of the room and is beginning to wilt, what is an opposite accommodation you can provide for the plant in order to make it stronger?

-If your younger sister or brother has taken one of your toys and you hit him/her, he/she will probably cry. What would have been an opposite response to that situation in order to avoid hurting your younger sibling?

-If you have a set of blocks, you might try building something that is tall and narrow. The next time you build something, what would be an opposite kind of structure you might design?

-If your shadow is longer in the early morning and the late afternoon when the sun is low in the sky, what can you predict about the length of your shadow at 1 p.m. when the sun is high in the sky?

-If the mercury of a thermometer rises when it is hot, can you predict what it will do when it is cold?

What different solutions can solve the problem?

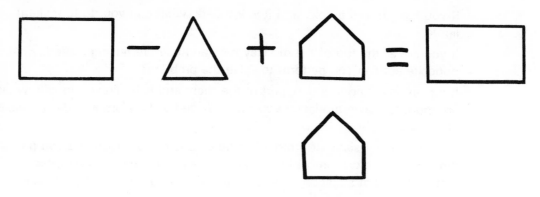

Add more ideas. Use the other side.

ill. 41

What different solutions can solve the problem?

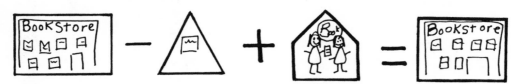

Marta age 5½

Add more ideas. Use the other side.

ill. 42

CAN YOU THINK OF A VARIETY OF SUBSTITUTES FOR CREAM CHEESE IN SOLVING THE PROBLEM OF MAKING STUFFED CELERY STALKS?

THINKING PROCESSES UTILIZED

Critical Thinking:
-analyzing a problem in many different ways

Creative Thinking:
-substituting ingredients to create a new product and to solve a problem
-developing the potential to be fluent, flexible and original thinkers by creating a variety of original ingredients for a recipe

Logic:
-solving cause and effect relationships

Problem Solving:
-evaluating a problem
-collecting information to see what materials are available to solve a particular problem

MATERIALS AND EQUIPMENT

Ingredients:
-celery
-other ingredients suggested by children

Utensils:
-This will depend upon the children's suggestions.

Other Preparation:
-an experience chart - or a small sheet of paper if you are working with an individual child
-a diagram for each child (see ill. 41)

PRE-COOKING ACTIVITIES

ACTIVITY #1 *Analyze and evaluate a problem.*

> -We are going to make our own hors d'oeuvres.
> We are going to fill some of the celery stalks with cream cheese.
>
> -Why do you think it might be a good idea to substitute the cream cheese filling with other ingredients in some of the other celery stalks?

ACTIVITY #2 *Substitute ingredients.*

> -Why is cream cheese considered a good filling for celery stalks?
>
> -List all the ingredients you might substitute for cream cheese.
> Justify the selection of those ingredients.
> (List the children's responses.)

COOKING SUGGESTIONS

-Arrange the suggested ingredients on separate plates.
Children form a line.
They collect the ingredients they need to fill two or three celery stalks in different ways.

POST-COOKING ACTIVITIES

ACTIVITY #1 *Solve other problems by using the process of substitution.*

> (The following problems can be done as a class, in small groups or individually. Answers may be recorded in diagram form as in ill. 41.)
>
> -If you didn't have enough money to go to the movies, what could you have substituted for going to the movies?
>
> -If you wanted to take a telephone message and didn't have a pencil, what could you have substituted for the pencil?
>
> -If the bookstore in your neighborhood were out of the book you wanted, what other solutions could you have arrived at in order to have obtained the book (see ill. 42)?

ACTIVITY #2 *Solve problems in specific curricular areas using the process of substitution.*

-Examine this diagram:

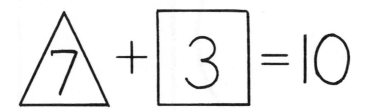

What other numerals can you substitute for the seven and the three in order to make the number sentence true?

-Proofread a story you have written.
If you have used the same adjective more than once, substitute the duplicated adjective with a different word that means the same thing or conveys the same idea.

-Explore all the different energy sources scientists might investigate to substitute for oil.

-Design an experiment to see the effects water has on sugar.
Compare the effects water has on other ingredients by substituting sugar with other substances.

-If you are trying to read a new word in a sentence, guess the word after examining how it begins and ends, and after reading the rest of the sentence.
If that word doesn't make sense, substitute it with different words that begin and end like that one, until you find the word that fits best.

-Hypothesize about how trilobites might have become extinct. Some scientists think that the water temperature might have changed.
Substitute other ideas for that one.

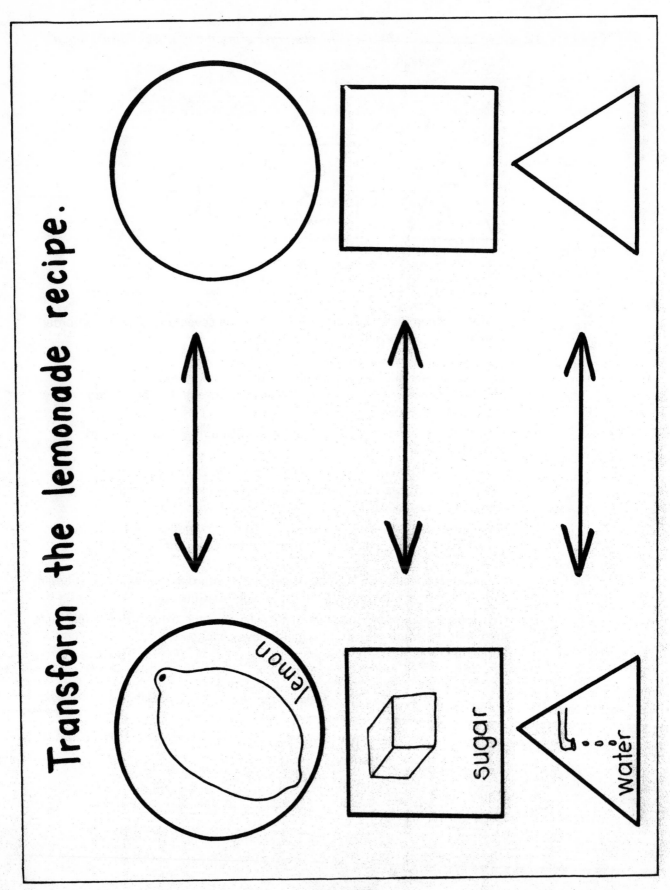

ill. 43

CAN YOU TRANSFORM A LEMONADE RECIPE BY SUBSTITUTING DIFFERENT INGREDIENTS?

THINKING PROCESSES UTILIZED

Critical Thinking:
-classifying ingredients in order to make substitutions
-comparing ingredients and finished products

Creative Thinking:
-substituting one idea for another to transform a product or a situation

Logic:
-predicting the results of the transformations
-making inferences from previous experiences in order to make substitutions in a new plan
-seeing cause and effect relationships as a result of substitutions

Problem Solving:
-evaluating the newly created product or situation to see if it meets the necessary criteria
-defining the problem before making substitutions

MATERIALS AND EQUIPMENT

Ingredients:
-lemon
-sugar
-water

Utensils:
-cups
-measuring spoons

Other preparation:
-a prepared lemonade recipe (see COOKING SUGGESTIONS)
-experience chart paper (or a small sheet of paper for an individual experience)
-a diagram for each child (see ill. 43)

PRE-COOKING ACTIVITIES

ACTIVITY #1 *Analyze the ingredients and the lemonade recipe.*

-Examine the ingredients in lemonade.

-Describe the taste of each ingredient.

-Read the recipe to see how much of each ingredient is needed.

-Predict the taste of the drink.

COOKING SUGGESTIONS:

This is a lemonade recipe for an individual child to make:

-PUT 2½ t of fresh lemon juice in an empty paper cup.
-ADD 1t of sugar.
-ADD cold water to fill the cup.
-STIR and DRINK.

POST-COOKING ACTIVITIES

ACTIVITY #1 *Evaluate the lemonade.*

-How did the drink taste?

-Did it taste the way you predicted it would?

-How would you have changed the drink to make it more to your liking?

ACTIVITY #2 *Classify the ingredients.*
(Record the children's responses.)

-List foods that are like sugar.

-List foods that are like lemon.

-List foods that are like water.

ACTIVITY #3 *Substitute ingredients.*

-If you wanted to make a similar drink to lemonade, but you wanted to change the ingredients, what foods would you substitute for the sugar, the lemon and the water?

-What information do you have to consider before making the substitutions?

ACTIVITY #4 *Record the substitutions.*

-Use the diagram in illustration 43 to record substitutions for the original ingredients.

COOKING SUGGESTIONS

-The lemonade and the newly created drink may either be prepared at the same time or as part of two separate experiences.

-A comparison of the two drinks might be easier for younger children to make if the drinks are prepared at the same time.
In this way they can also see a one-to-one correspondence of ingredients.

POST-COOKING ACTIVITIES

ACTIVITY #1 *Compare the lemonade and the newly created drink.*

-Did the substituted ingredients create a drink similar to the lemonade?

-How was the second drink the same as the lemonade?
How was it different?

ACTIVITY #2 *Extend the concept of substitution to other situations.*

-Substitute one event for another in a particular story to see how a different event might have changed the outcome.

-Substitute one measure of music for another to see the effect on the entire piece of music.

-Substitute three blocks for one block in one of your buildings.

-Substitute going on a see-saw with an equivalent activity.

-Substitute paper clips for equivalent objects in a study on magnets.

HOW CAN YOU REDESIGN A BOLOGNA, CHEESE AND OLIVE PLATTER?

THINKING PROCESSES UTILIZED

Critical Thinking:
-classifying ingredients

Creative Thinking:
-redesigning to create something new

Logic:
-recognizing cause and effect relationships in redesigning something

Problem Solving:
-defining problems
-evaluating various solutions to a problem

MATERIALS AND EQUIPMENT

Ingredients:
-bologna
-cheese
-olives
-ingredients suggested by children

Utensils:
-a platter
-individual plates
-knives
-forks
-other utensils suggested by children

Other Preparation:
-a simulated bologna, cheese, olive platter made from felt, construction paper or magazine clippings
-drawing paper
-crayons or markers
-chart paper or a small sheet of paper depending upon the size of the group

PRE-COOKING ACTIVITIES

ACTIVITY #1 *Define the problems.*

-We are going to prepare a bologna, cheese and olive platter next week.

-Display the simulated platter with a simple arrangement of the ingredients. This is one way the platter can be designed.

-Let's think about ways to redesign the platter to make it as attractive as possible.
You may include additional ingredients to enhance the platter in one or more ways.

-Can you redesign the platter by manipulating the simulated ingredients, by suggesting additional ingredients, or by creating your own ideas?

ACTIVITY #2 *Record a design.*

-Redesign the original platter.
Record your ideas on drawing paper.
You can do several different designs.
Share your favorite design.

ACTIVITY #3 *Evaluate the designs.*

-Encourage each child to share his/her ideas regarding the rationale behind the final design.

-What are the criteria we should use in evaluating the designs?

-Prepare one of the designs.

COOKING SUGGESTIONS

If the children have the appropriate skills, they can estimate the amount of food to purchase.

POST-COOKING ACTIVITIES

ACTIVITY #1 *Define problems in redesigning something.*

-What are the problems you have to consider before you redesign something in your environment?
List the children's responses.

-What are the different ways you can redesign something?
List the children's responses.

ACTIVITY #2 *Apply the criteria for redesigning something to real situations.*

-If you were redesigning a lunch box, which of the problems you listed would you have to consider?

-Are there additional problems that were not listed?
Add them.

-Using some of the ways you can redesign something, create a new design for a lunch box.
Record it on paper.

ACTIVITY #3 *Extend the idea of redesigning to specific content areas.*

-Give each child two lists with which to work.
One should include the problems involved in redesigning something.
The other one should include the methods you can use to redesign something.
The lists can be recorded as symbols rather than as sentences.

-Redesign the exterior of an old building so it looks more modern.
Use both lists to help you.
Put an X next to the problems you have to consider.
Put an X next to the methods you might use in redesigning the building.
Did you have to add new ideas to the lists?

-Redesign Columbus' voyage in order to help him land in the country he included in his plans.
Use both lists to help you.

-Redesign your room.
Use both lists to help you.

-Design an experiment that measures the effects of water on plants.
Redesign the experiment to discover the effects of light on plants.
Use both lists.
If necessary, continue to add new ideas to the lists.

-Redesign one of your favorite toys or games.
Use both lists.

-Redesign a friendship you have with one of your friends.
Use both lists.

67

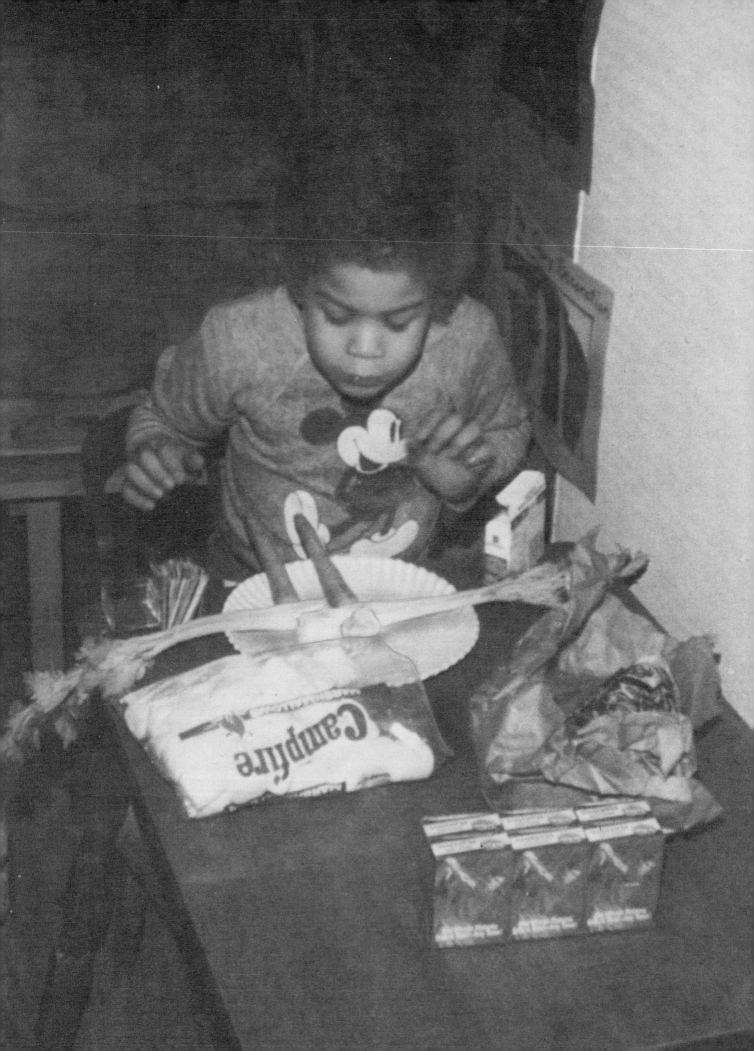

CAN YOU DEFINE THE PROBLEMS YOU HAVE TO SOLVE BEFORE YOU CAN BUILD A ROBOT YOU CAN EAT?

THINKING PROCESSES UTILIZED

Critical Thinking:
-analyzing problems to arrive at a solution

Creative Thinking:
-combining ingredients to create an original idea

Logic:
-developing a strategy to build the final product

Problem Solving:
-defining problems to clarify and organize a situation
-evaluating the ingredients

MATERIALS AND EQUIPMENT

Ingredients and Utensils:
This will depend upon the children's suggestions.

Other Preparation:
-an experience chart (A smaller sheet of paper can be used if you are working with one or two children.)
-drawing paper
-markers or crayons

PRE-COOKING ACTIVITIES

ACTIVITY #1 *Define problems.*
-What questions will you need to answer before you can build a robot you can eat?
Record children's responses.

ACTIVITY #2 *Design your robot.*

(These activities are based on problems the child might have suggested in ACTIVITY #1.)

-Draw a picture of the robot you have in mind.
 Avoid making a junk food robot.

-Label the ingredients.

-Do the foods you selected go well together?

-Change the ingredients that don't go well together.

-How will the ingredients stay together without using glue?

-What other materials will we need?

COOKING SUGGESTIONS

-Each child can bring the necessary ingredients for his/her robot from home.

-The idea of building a robot can be substituted by having the child build anything that represents his/her interests or special area of study.

-This cooking experience can be done as an art project.

POST-COOKING ACTIVITIES

ACTIVITY #1 *Develop the skill of defining problems in other situations.*

(This will depend upon the child's interests and what he/she is studying.)

-How many different ways can you make a puppet?
 What problems do you have to consider before you make it?

-If you are planning to take a trip, what are all the problems you have to solve before you take it?

-Measure the area of your living room floor.
 What problems do you have to consider before you begin to measure?

-Select an animal you would like to study first-hand.
 What questions do you have to think about before you begin your study?

-What are the problems you have to consider while playing a game of chess?

WHAT IS THE DIFFERENCE BETWEEN A FRUIT SALAD AND A POTATO PANCAKE?

THINKING PROCESSES UTILIZED

Critical Thinking:
-comparing and contrasting the difference between two finished products

Creative Thinking:
-transforming a product by changing the process applied to it
-brainstorming in order to arrive at many different solutions to a problem

Logic:
-recognizing the effect of various processes on a final product
-recognizing the effect of a specific combination of ingredients on a final product
-making predictions about the effects of different processes on different products

Problem Solving:
-defining problems in order to make changes
-analyzing information to arrive at a solution

MATERIALS AND EQUIPMENT

Ingredients:
-potatoes
-eggs
-all-purpose flour
-onions
-salt
-oil
-applesauce

Utensils:
-grater
-knives
-cutting boards
-electric or regular frying pan
-stove or hot plate
-plates

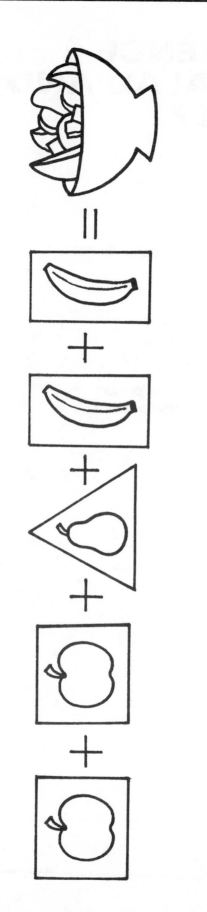

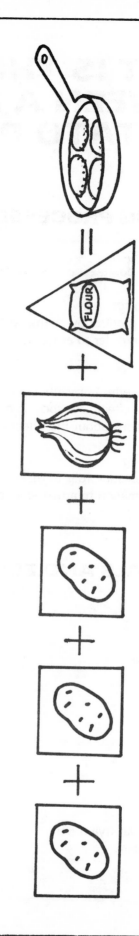

Compare the fruit salad recipe with the potato pancake recipe.

ill. 44

-mixing bowls
-spoons
-spatula
-a sifter

Other Preparation:
-experience chart paper (or a small sheet of paper - depending upon the size of the group)
-a large copy of the diagram seen in illustration 44
-individual copies of the diagram seen in illustration 45

PRE-COOKING ACTIVITIES

ACTIVITY #1 *Compare the fruit salad and potato pancake recipes.*

-Examine the large diagram of the fruit salad recipe and the potato pancake recipe (see ill. 44).

-Examine the ingredients and how they are recorded.

-How are the recipes the same?

-How are the recipes different?

ACTIVITY #2 *Analyze the comparisons of the two recipes.*

-List the reasons the final products are different.

ACTIVITY #3 *Transform the original fruit salad.*

-Change the original fruit salad by changing the products and the processes.

-Prepare a plan for a new fruit salad.
 For example:

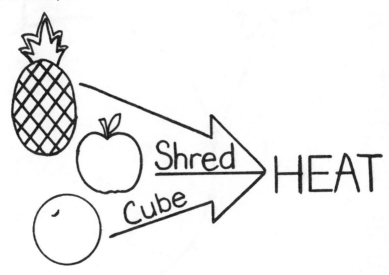

-Predict the effects the changed processes will have on the final product.

Choose a product.
List as many different processes as you can
think of that will affect the product.

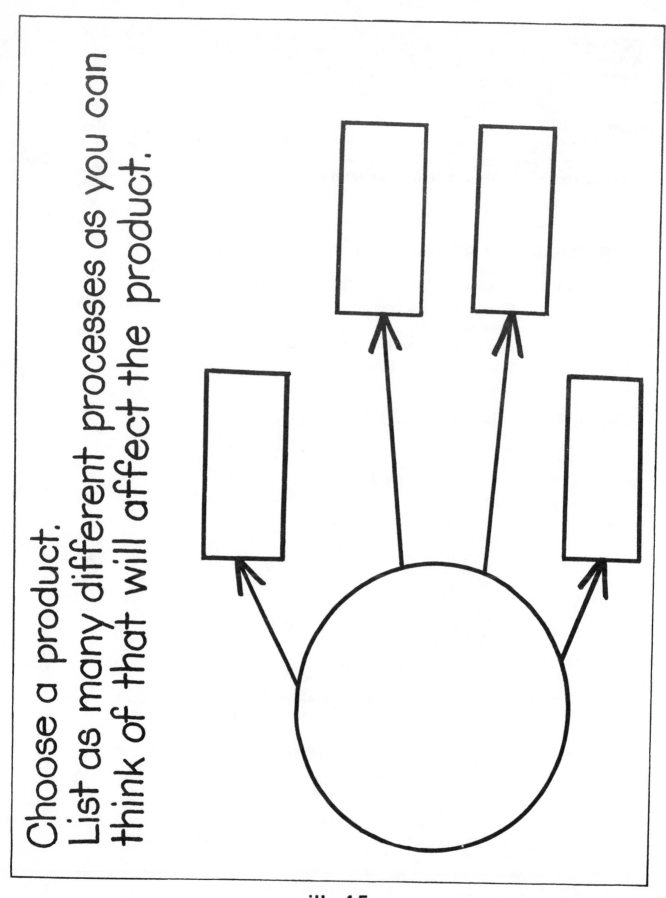

ill. 45

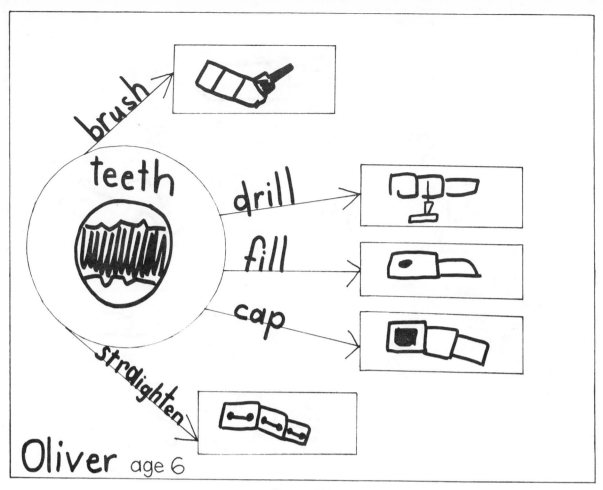

brush teeth drill fill cap straighten

Oliver age 6

ill. 46

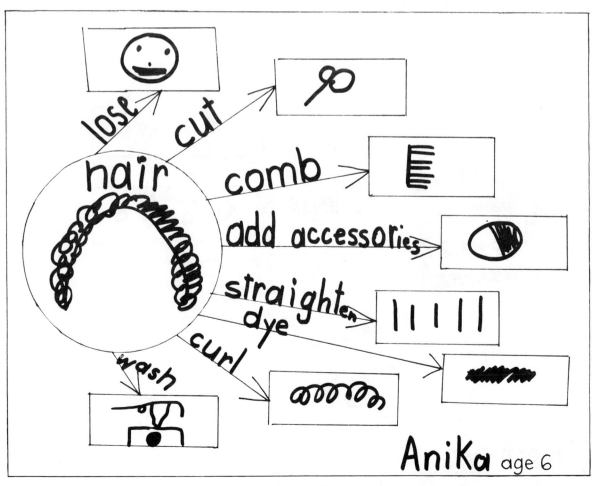

lose cut hair comb add accessories straighten dye curl wash

Anika age 6

ill. 47

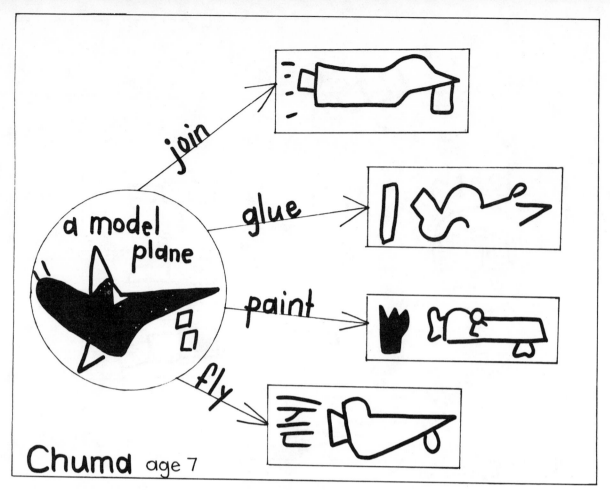

ill. 48

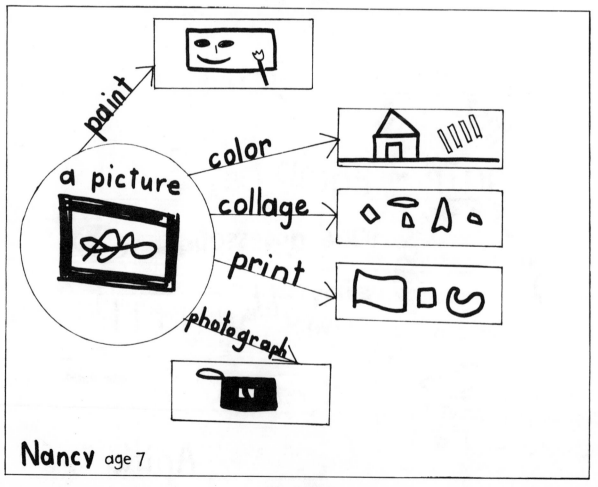

ill. 49

COOKING SUGGESTIONS

-Call attention to the specific processes as you cook with the children.

-Build the words "process" and "product" into the children's vocabulary.

-The preparation of each recipe may be done as two separate experiences.

-The following recipe makes approximately twelve potato pancakes:

    -START with 2 cups of pared and grated potatoes.
    -BEAT 3 eggs.
    -STIR the eggs into the grated potatoes.
    -COMBINE and SIFT 1 ½ t of all-purpose flour and 1 1/4t of salt.
    -ADD the flour to the potato mixture.
    -ADD 2t of grated onion.
    -STIR.
    -HEAT ¼ inch of oil in a pan.
    -SPOON the mixture into the pan of hot oil to make 3 inch diameter pancakes.
    -BROWN until crisp on both sides.
    -SERVE hot with applesauce.

POST-COOKING ACTIVITIES

ACTIVITY #1 *Recognize the effect other processes have on final products.*

    -What are all the different processes you can think of that will affect a flower?

    -What are all the different processes you can think of that will affect a picture?

ACTIVITY #2 *Record the effect of different processes on different products.*

    -Children record their ideas on individual diagrams (see ills. 46, 47, 48 & 49).

ACTIVITY #3 *Identify and select various processes to solve specific problems.*
(This will depend upon what the child is studying and his particular interests.)

    -Experiment with wires, batteries and bulbs.
    What are all the different processes you must perform in order for the bulb to light up?

    -When an author writes a story, what are all the ways he/she can show the reader that a character in the story is angry?

    -What are all the different processes you can apply to a piece of paper to change its shape?

    -What processes must be performed in caring for a vegetable garden?

    -What processes do you have to perform in order to get ready for bed?

Plan a fruit dish that requires heat.

Process	Ingredient	Process
BAKE	banana	Peel cut
	Cinnamon	Sprinkle
	sugar	Sprinkle

Ali age 6

ill. 50

IF THE PROCESS OF HEATING MAKES FRUIT SOFT, CAN YOU CREATE A FRUIT DESSERT OR SIDE DISH THAT MIGHT TASTE GOOD AFTER IT IS HEATED?

THINKING PROCESSES UTILIZED

Critical Thinking:
-comparing different processes in order to plan a product

Creative Thinking:
-risk taking to encourage the creation of unusual and original ideas

Logic:
-making predictions in selecting ingredients
-making inferences and deductions from previous experiences and data in order to collect new
 information and to create original ideas
-recognizing cause and effect relationships and patterns to gain a better understanding of the
 processes involved

Problem Solving:
-collecting data to make inferences and deductions
-solution finding by making deductions and inferences

MATERIALS AND EQUIPMENT

Ingredients and Utensils:
-This will depend upon the children's suggested ingredients and recipes

Other Preparation:
-chart paper or a small sheet of paper depending upon the size of the group
-a duplicated diagram for each child (see ill. 51)

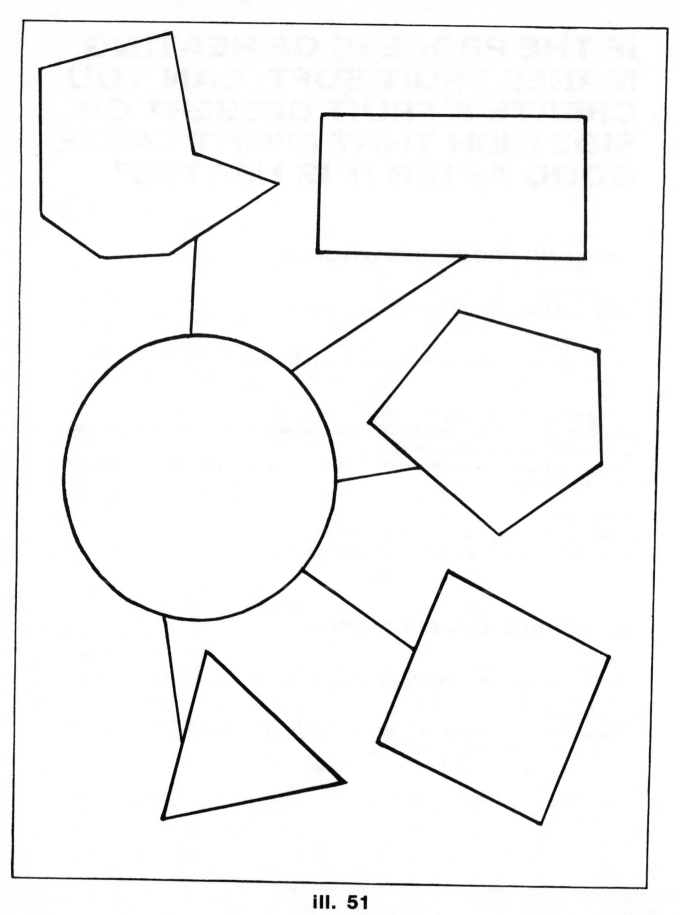

ill. 51

PRE-COOKING ACTIVITIES

ACTIVITY #1 *List different methods of heating.*
Compare them.

-What are all the different ways fruit can be heated?
Record children's responses.

-Compare the results of baking, frying, broiling, boiling, simmering and roasting fruit.

-What can you infer about the effect of heat on fruit?

ACTIVITY #2 *Plan a recipe.*

-Choose a fruit that might taste good after it is heated.

-How would you like to heat it?

-What other processes will you perform on the fruit before you heat it?

-Think of other ingredients you might add before you heat it.

-Are there additional ingredients you would like to add after you heat it?

-Plan your dessert in diagram form (see ill. 50).

COOKING SUGGESTIONS

Encourage children to prepare a recipe with a fruit that they normally don't like raw. This will help strengthen their sense of risk taking.

POST-COOKING ACTIVITIES

ACTIVITY #1 *Make deductions to gather more information.*
Make inductions to create new ideas.

This will depend upon the topics the children are studying.

-If a mammal is an animal that bears its young live, nurses its young and is covered with fur, list all the animals at your local zoo that are mammals and predict the kind of environment in which they would be best suited (see ill. 52).

-If numerals with final digits of 0, 2, 4, 6 and 8 represent even numbers, what are all the even numbers between 25 and 63?
Examine the list and decide other attributes these even numbers have in common.

-If words that end with the same last syllable usually rhyme, list as many words as you can that rhyme with vacation.
Can you write other sets of words that rhyme (see ill. 53)?

-If 2/2 (or two halves) of a cupcake can be divided equally between two

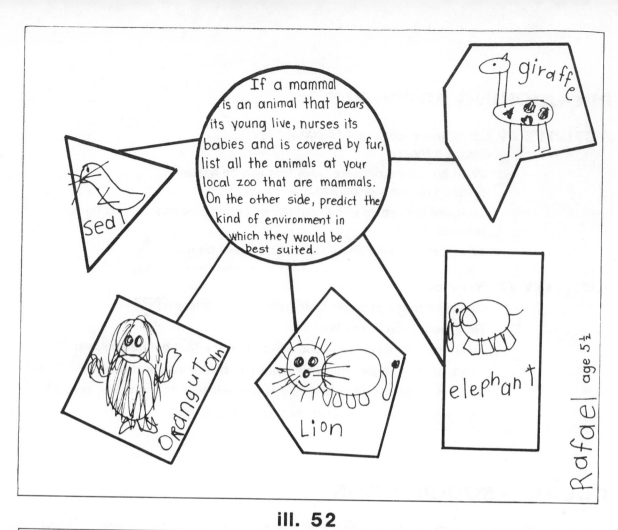

If a mammal is an animal that bears its young live, nurses its babies and is covered by fur, list all the animals at your local zoo that are mammals. On the other side, predict the kind of environment in which they would be best suited.

giraffe

Sed

Orangutan

Lion

elephant

Rafael age 5½

ill. 52

If words that end with the same last syllable usually rhyme, list as many words as you can that rhyme with <u>vacation</u>.

transportation

animation

fascination

sanitation

communication

Ruby age 7

ill. 53

people, 3/3 (or three thirds) of a cupcake can be divided equally among three people, then how many ?/4 (or ? fourths) of a cupcake can be divided equally among four people?
Can you continue the pattern?

-If people use sponges, rags, paper towels and newsprint to clean spilled liquids, what properties do you think each of the materials has in common?

-If an architect considers the function of a building in designing its shape, what shapes might he use in designing a school?

List the processes you can apply to each ingredient in order to prepare the pizza.

cut or tear ⟶ English muffin

pour or spoon ⟶ Ragu Pizza Sauce

cut or shred ⟶ Mozzarella cheese

sprinkle ⟶ Parmesian cheese

sprinkle or shake ⟶ Oregano

ill. 54

CAN YOU PREDICT WHAT WILL HAPPEN TO DIFFERENT PIZZA INGREDIENTS AFTER THEY HAVE BEEN BAKED IN AN OVEN?

THINKING PROCESSES UTILIZED

Critical Thinking:
-analyzing information in order to solve a problem
-classifying different products according to how they are affected by a specific process

Logic:
-making predictions about how a process will affect a product
-making deductions and inferences after making observations
-observing cause and effect relationships

Problem Solving:
-collecting information in order to prepare the product
-observing the effect of the same process on different products
-validating predictions

MATERIALS AND EQUIPMENT

Ingredients:
-English muffins
-canned or bottled pizza sauce
-mozzarella cheese
-parmesian cheese
-oregano

Utensils:
-portable or regular oven
-spoon or ladle
-knife
-cutting board

How was each pizza ingredient affected by the heating process?

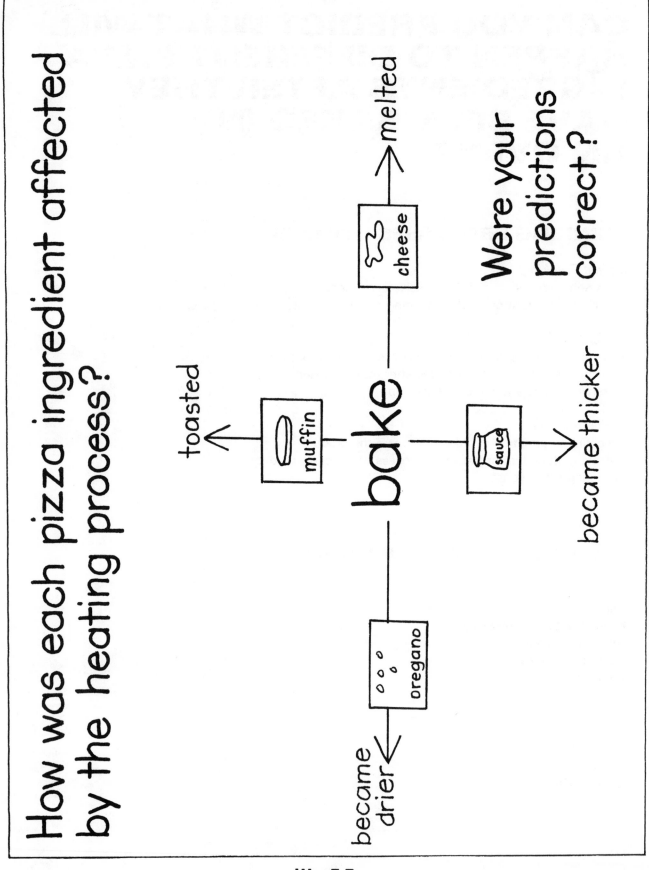

oregano → became drier

muffin → toasted

bake

cheese → melted

sauce → became thicker

Were your predictions correct?

ill. 55

Other Preparation:
-blank diagrams, or chart paper or small sheet of paper depending upon the size of the group (see samples of completed diagram in ills. 54, 55 & 56)
-an experience chart (A small sheet of paper can be used if you are working with one or two children.)

PRE-COOKING ACTIVITIES

ACTIVITY #1 *Collect information.*

-Look in different cookbooks for pizza recipes.

-Choose one you like best.

-List the ingredients you will need.

-List the utensils you will need.

-Predict what will happen to each ingredient after it is baked.

-Record the children's suggestions (see ill. 54).

COOKING SUGGESTIONS:

The ingredients listed under MATERIALS AND EQUIPMENT can be used in a simple preparation of pizza which each child can prepare himself/herself:

CUT each muffin in half.
ADD a tablespoon or more of the sauce to each half.
ADD shredded or diced mozzarella cheese to each half.
SPRINKLE with parmesan cheese and oregano.
HEAT in a 350 degree oven.
CHECK the pizza in five minutes.
THINK: If the pizza is not ready, what do you think you should do?

POST-COOKING SUGGESTIONS

ACTIVITY #1 *Validate predictions.*

-How was each pizza ingredient affected by the heating process? Record the children's responses (see ill. 55).

-Were your predictions correct about how heat would affect the different ingredients?

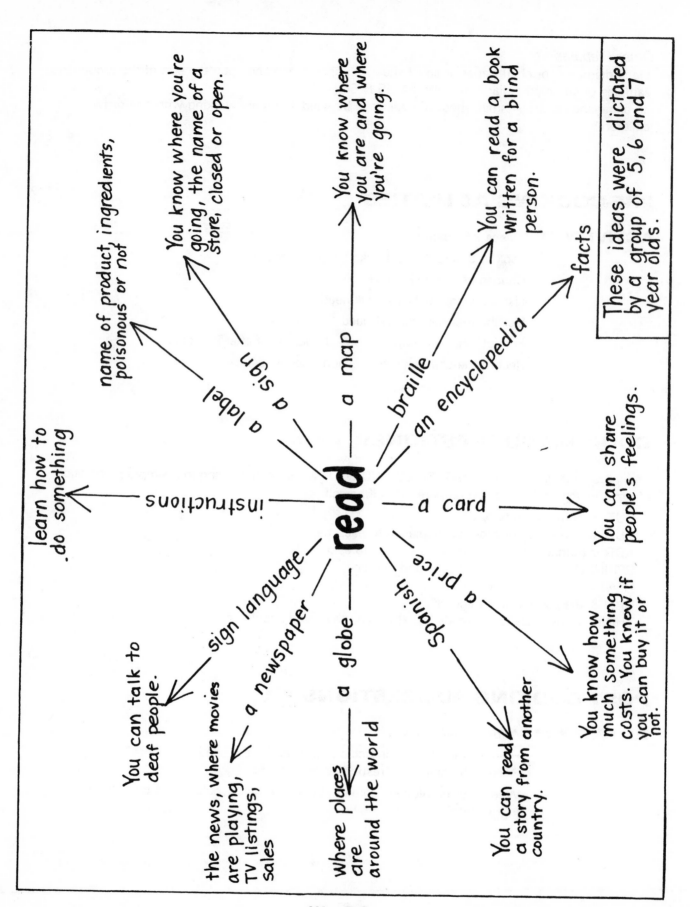

read

a map — You know where you are and where you're going.

a sign — You know where you're going, the name of a store, closed or open.

a label — name of product, ingredients, poisonous or not

instructions — learn how to do something

sign language — You can talk to deaf people.

a newspaper — the news, where movies are playing, TV listings, sales

a globe — Where places are around the world

Spanish — You can read a story from another country.

a price — You know how much something costs. You know if you can buy it or not.

a card — You can share people's feelings.

braille — You can read a book written for a blind person.

an encyclopedia — facts

These ideas were dictated by a group of 5, 6 and 7 year olds.

ill. 56

ACTIVITY #2 *Discover other process-product relationships.*

-Choose a process.

-List as many different products that can be affected by the process.

-List the effect of the same process on the different products. Record the children's suggestions in diagram form (see ill. 56).

ACTIVITY #3 *Analyze the effect of a specific process on different products.*
(This will depend upon the child's interests and upon what he/she is studying.)

-Compare the effects of creating a magnetic field around a pin, a sheet of paper, a screw, a bottle cap, etc.

-Compare the effects of blowing on a hot piece of food, blowing on a lit candle, blowing on a piece of paper and blowing on a pinwheel.

-Compare the effects of brushing hair, brushing teeth, brushing paint, etc.

-Compare the effects of stuffing a turkey, stuffing a pillow, stuffing a suitcase, and ''stuffing yourself.''

-Compare the effects of writing a letter, writing a book, writing a song, and writing a check.

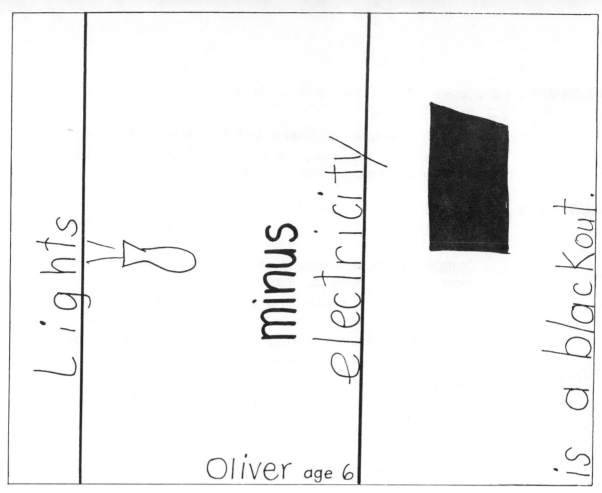

Lights

minus

electricity

is a blackout.

Oliver age 6

ill. 57

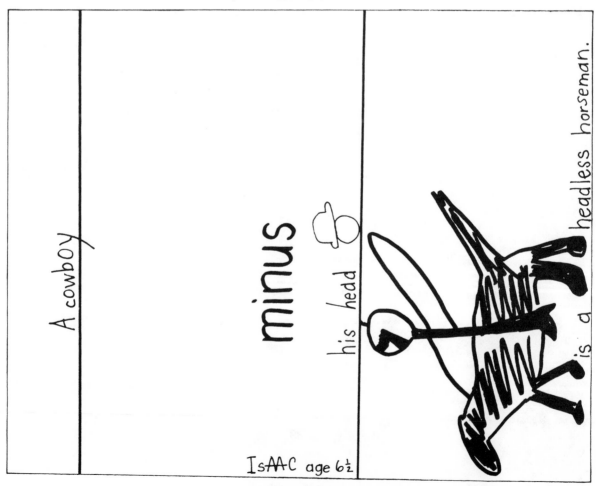

A cowboy

minus

his head

is a headless horseman.

Isaac age 6½

ill. 58

WHAT WOULD HAPPEN IF YOU SUBTRACTED WATER FROM A GELATIN DESSERT?

THINKING PROCESSES UTILIZED

Critical Thinking:
-analyzing the relationship of parts to wholes

Creative Thinking:
-subtracting to create something different

Logic:
-recognizing cause and effect relationships

Problem Solving:
-predicting the results of subtracting an element from a product or a situation

MATERIALS AND EQUIPMENT

Ingredients:
-½ cup of water
-1 package of plain gelatin
-1 six ounce can of any frozen juice except pineapple juice
-¼ cup of honey

Utensils:
-a measuring cup
-a pot
-a hot plate or range
-a mixing bowl
-a mixing spoon
-cups
-spoons

Other Preparation:
-reproduced diagrams for each child (See ills. 57, 58, 59 & 60 for completed samples.)
-crayons, markers and/or pencils

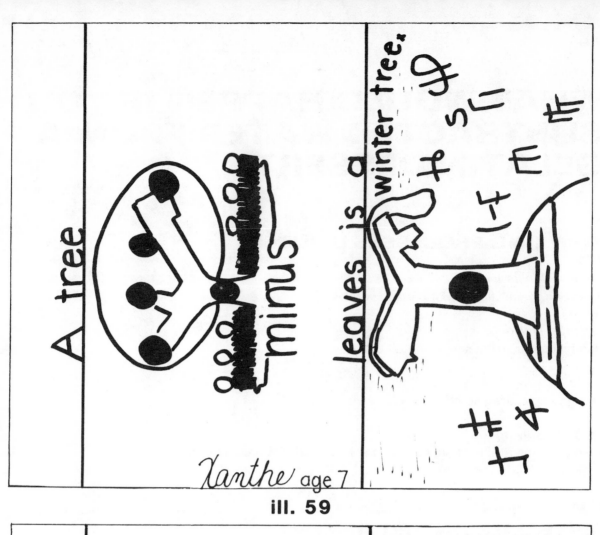

A tree minus leaves is a winter tree.

Xanthe age 7

ill. 59

A tv minus its screen is a radio.

Jacob age 6½

ill. 60

PRE-COOKING ACTIVITIES

ACTIVITY #1 *Dissect the recipe.*

-Examine the ingredients and the processes in the gelatin dessert recipe (see COOKING SUGGESTIONS).

-What is the purpose of adding each of the ingredients?

-What is the purpose of performing each of the processes?

-Predict the outcome of the combination of the above ingredients and processes.
Give reasons to support your predictions.

ACTIVITY #2 *Recognize cause and effect relationships.*

-What might happen if we eliminated water from the recipe? the gelatin? the frozen juice? the honey?
How would the subtraction of any of the ingredients change the dessert?

-How would the elimination of one or two of the processes change the dessert? (If possible, allow the children to experiment.)

COOKING SUGGESTIONS

The following is a simple gelatin recipe that serves six:

COMBINE ½ cup of cold water and one package of plain gelatin.
COOK and STIR the water and the gelatin over low heat until the gelatin is completely dissolved.
REMOVE the pan from the stove or hot plate.
ADD and STIR a six ounce can of frozen juice (not pineapple), one cup of cold water and ¼ cup of honey.
POUR the mixture into a bowl.
REFRIGERATE until the mixture jells (about two hours).

-If you are cooking with a large group you can make two or three different flavored desserts.

-Children can add fruits, nuts and/or whipped cream to their desserts.

POST-COOKING ACTIVITIES

ACTIVITY #1 *Introduce the idea of subtraction into specific content areas or daily experiences.*

-Defrost the freezer in your refrigerator.
What happened to the items in the freezer as the temperature became warmer? (This can also be done by taking an item from the freezer and placing it in another part of the refrigerator or by removing it from the refrigerator.)

-Subtract the final "e" from each of the following words: cane   wine   site
 Can you read the new words?

-Subtract red from purple.
 What color did you get?

-Go to the store with 50 cents.
 Buy something that costs a dime. How much money will you have left?

-Subtract one of the characters from a story.
 How would it change the story?

-What would happen to a rainbow if the sun began to hide behind the
 clouds?

-What would happen if you lost a glove in the middle of winter?

ACTIVITY #2 *Begin to recognize the results of subtraction in familiar situations.*

-Think of an object or a situation.
 Take one thing away from it.
 How will the object or situation change?
 Record your ideas in diagram form (see ills. 57, 58, 59 & 60).

HOW CAN YOU CHANGE CHOCOLATE MILK INTO SOMETHING ELSE YOU CAN DRINK OR EAT?

THINKING PROCESSES UTILIZED

Critical Thinking:
-comparing and contrasting to analyze products and processes

Creative Thinking:
-adding ingredients to improve the recipe
-brainstorming to develop divergent thinking skills

Logic:
-discovering cause and effect relationships

Problem Solving:
-justifying the addition of various ingredients to a recipe
-predicting the effects of various cooking processes on different ingredients

MATERIALS AND EQUIPMENT

Ingredients:
-powdered chocolate
-milk
-whipped cream (Home-made is the best!)
-chocolate chips
-cookies
-marshmallows

Utensils:
-cups
-spoons
-a pot
-a hot plate or stove
-an ice-cube tray
-a ladle or large spoon
-a bowl

-aluminum foil
-popsicle sticks

Other Preparation:
-drawing paper
-crayons, markers and/or pencils
-individual copies of the diagram in ill. 65
-a list of ingredients (see PRE-COOKING ACTIVITY #2)

PRE-COOKING ACTIVITIES

ACTIVITY #1 *Compare a hot chocolate and a chocolate milk recipe.*

-What ingredients do you combine and what processes do you use to make chocolate milk?

-What ingredients do you combine and what processes do you use to make hot chocolate?

-How are the two drinks the same?
 How are they different?

-Children respond orally.
 In addition they may record their responses by drawing a picture or by writing (see ills. 61, 62, 63 & 64).

ACTIVITY #2 *Justify adding or not adding different ingredients to hot chocolate.*

-Examine the list of ingredients:
 (Read the list to children who cannot read.)
      an ice-cube, a marshmallow, ice-cream,
      a cinnamon stick, whipped cream, celery,
      chicken soup, chocolate chips, a cookie

-Which ingredients might you add to hot chocolate?

-Justify your suggestions.

-Why wouldn't you add each of the other ingredients?

COOKING SUGGESTIONS

-Use powdered chocolate and milk for an easy preparation of hot chocolate.

-Place whipped cream (The children can whip it themselves.), chocolate chips, cookies and marshmallows on the cooking table.

-Ask the children to include one or two of the above ingredients in their hot chocolate drinks. Examine the ingredients to see how they are affected by the heat.

-The children can use a ladle or a large spoon to help them pour the hot chocolate into their cups.

They're both sweet.

caroLine
age 6

ill. 61

Both have oxygen
and air.

Joseph age 5½

ill. 62

One you just drink. The other, you wait to drink.

Kyla age 6

ill. 63

One you make only with milk.

One you can use water or milk.

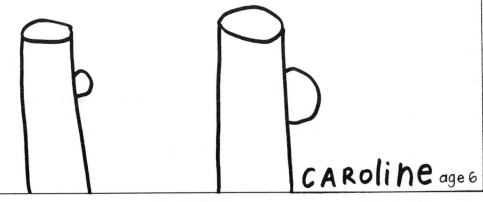

Caroline age 6

ill. 64

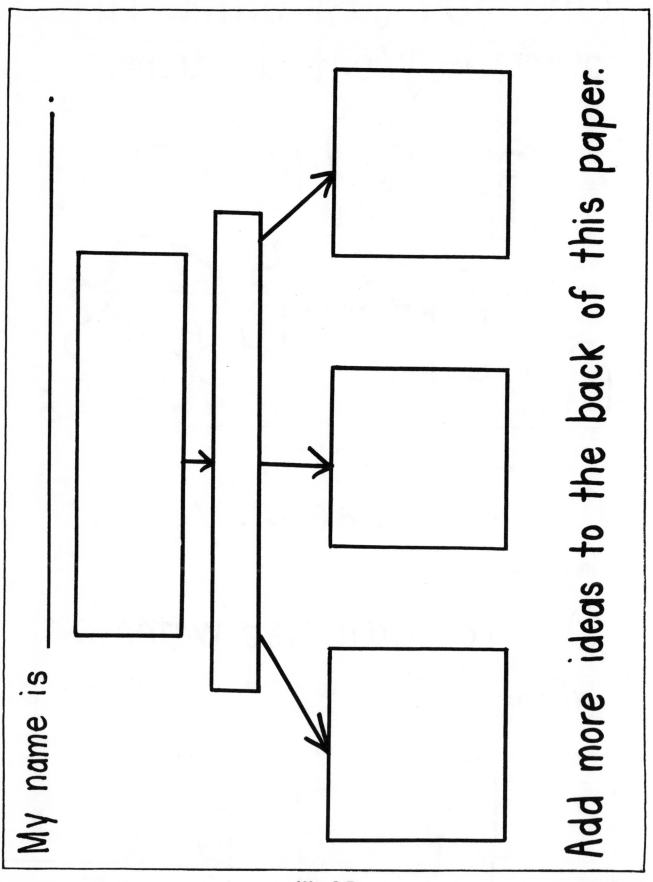

My name is _____.

Add more ideas to the back of this paper.

ill. 65

-In order to avoid a potential mess, have each child place his/her cup into a bowl as he/she pours the drink.

-Any spillage into the bowl can be poured back into the pot (see photo page 96).

POST-COOKING ACTIVITIES

ACTIVITY #1 *Examine the results of adding different ingredients to the hot chocolate. Predict the results of adding the same ingredients to a frozen chocolate milk recipe.*

-What happened to the chocolate chips, marshmallows, whipped cream and cookie when they were added to the hot chocolate?

-Predict what might happen to the same ingredients when they are combined to make frozen chocolate milk.

COOKING SUGGESTIONS

Here is a simple frozen chocolate milk recipe:

-PUT marshmallows in some of the ice-cube tray compartments, chips of cookies in some, etc. to compare the results.
-ADD chocolate milk.
-PLACE a piece of aluminum foil over the filled ice-cube tray.
-PLACE popsicle sticks through the aluminum foil and into each section of the ice-cube tray.
-FREEZE.

POST-COOKING ACTIVITIES

ACTIVITY #1 *Examine the results of adding different ingredients to frozen chocolate milk.*

-List what happened to each ingredient when it was added to hot chocolate.

-List what happened to each ingredient when it was added to frozen chocolate.

-Compare the results.

-Why do you think the results were different?

ACTIVITY #2 *Recognize similarities between each of the three recipes.*

-How are chocolate milk, hot chocolate and frozen chocolate milk the same?

ACTIVITY #3 *Develop the idea that something can satisfy the same purpose in many different ways.*

My name is __ANNe (age 6)_____.

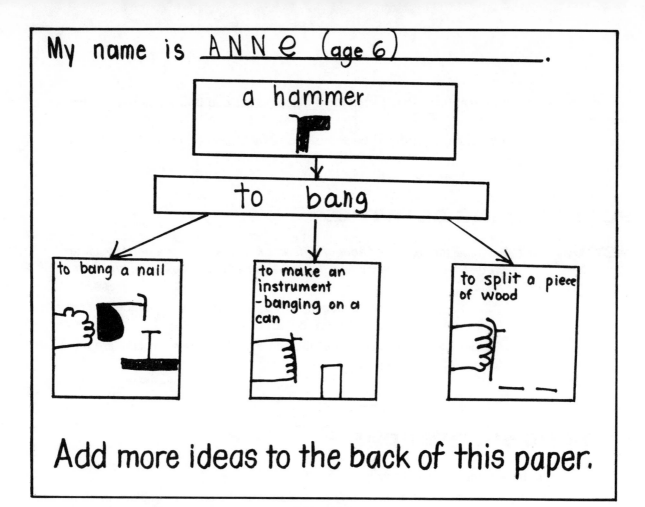

a hammer

↓

to bang

to bang a nail

to make an instrument —banging on a can

to split a piece of wood

Add more ideas to the back of this paper.

ill. 66

My name is __Raymond (age 7)_____.

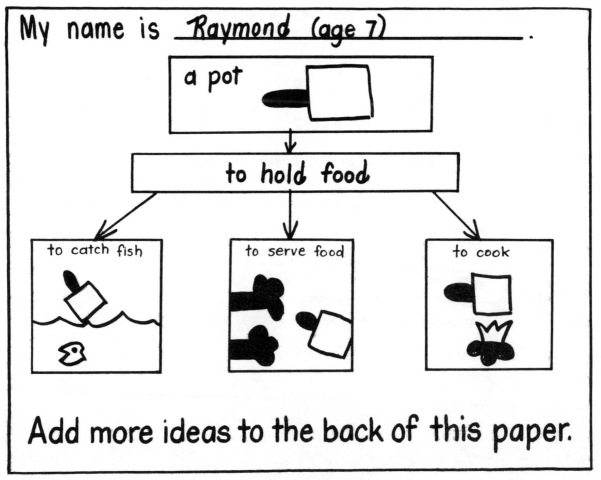

a pot

↓

to hold food

to catch fish

to serve food

to cook

Add more ideas to the back of this paper.

ill. 67

-What are the different ways you can use a ball for recreation?

-What are the different ways you can use a ribbon for decoration?

-What are the different ways you can use cards to teach you something?

ACTIVITY #4 *Work with a diagram (see ill. 65).*

-Select an object in the environment.

-Think of one of its purposes.

-How many different ways can you use the object so that it still has the same purpose?

-Record your responses in the diagram (see ills. 66 & 67).

Compare parts of a chicken to objects or situations in the environment with equivalent functions.

ill. 68

CAN YOU DISSECT A CHICKEN AND PREPARE DIFFERENT RECIPES FOR DIFFERENT PARTS OF THE CHICKEN?

THINKING PROCESSES UTILIZED

Critical Thinking:
-dissecting the whole in order to analyze the parts
-classifying various parts and seeing their relationship to the whole

Creative Thinking:
-regrouping chicken parts with other ingredients to form new recipes

Logic:
-making analogies to understand the function of various parts
-making inferences about the kinds of foods that can be prepared from the various chicken parts based on their characteristics

Problem Solving:
-collecting information to prepare different recipes

MATERIALS AND EQUIPMENT

Ingredients:
-a chicken
-other ingredients based on recipes collected by the children

Utensils:
-This will depend upon the recipes collected.

Other Preparation:
-knife, poultry shears or a picture of a cross section of a chicken
-an experience chart or small sheet of paper, depending upon the size of the group
-duplicated diagrams for each child (see ills. 68 & 69)

Choose an object or a situation.
Compare the functions of various parts to the functions of various parts of a bicycle.

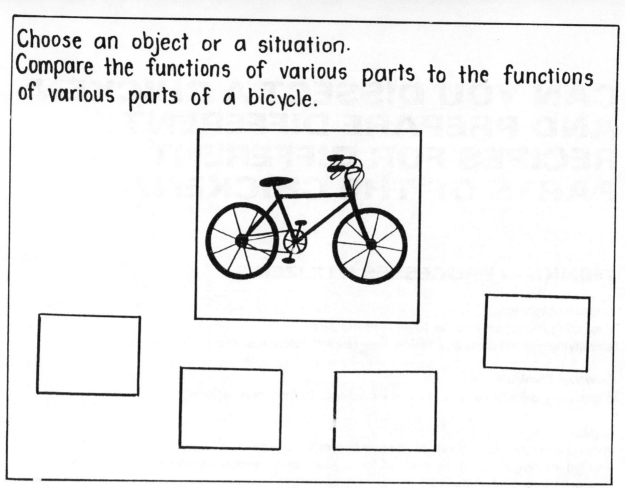

ill. 69

Choose an object or a situation.
Compare the functions of various parts to the functions of various parts of a bicycle.

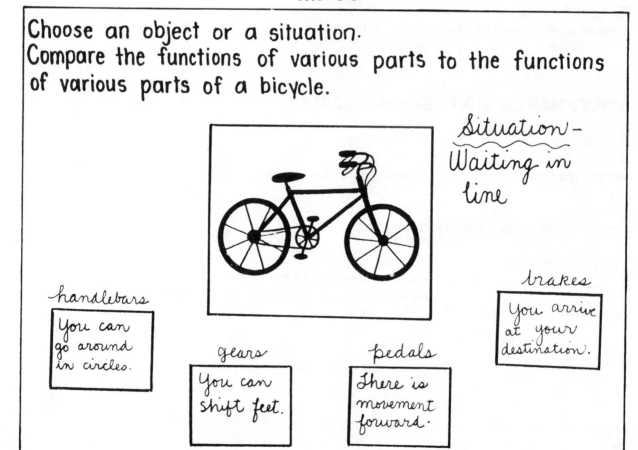

Situation —
Waiting in line

handlebars
You can go around in circles.

gears
You can shift feet.

pedals
There is movement forward.

brakes
You arrive at your destination.

Stacy & Svetlana age 9

ill. 70

PRE-COOKING ACTIVITIES

ACTIVITY #1 *Dissect the chicken.*

-This can be done with a knife, a poultry shears or by showing the class a picture of a cross section of a chicken.

-List the parts and their functions.
Record the children's responses on paper.

ACTIVITY #2 *Analyze the function of the parts to the whole.*

-Compare parts of a chicken to objects or situations in the environment with equivalent functions. (Use the diagram in ill. 68.)

ACTIVITY #3 *Predict different kinds of foods that can be prepared from different parts of the chicken.*

-Classify the different parts in different ways.

-Can you prepare the same kinds of food from the different parts of the chicken?

-Give examples of the different kinds of recipes that might be prepared with different parts of the chicken. (Ask children to name dishes based on their experiences with food.)

ACTIVITY #4 *Collect information.*

-Consult adults, friends and/or cookbooks to find recipes for different parts of the chicken.

COOKING SUGGESTIONS

This lesson can also be done with other foods that consist of parts that can be used in different ways.
Examples: a pumpkin, a fish, a lemon.

POST-COOKING ACTIVITIES

ACTIVITY #1 *Recognize relationships of parts to wholes.*

-Draw a picture of your bicycle or a friend's bicycle.

-Include all the parts you can see and all the parts you cannot usually see.

-Label the parts.

-How does each part help the bicycle?
(If you do not know, ask a friend to help you or consult a book.)

ACTIVITY #2 *Make analogies to further one's understanding of relationships.*

-Choose an object or a situation.

-Dissect it in your mind.

-List the various parts.

-What are the functions of the various parts?

-Compare the functions of the various parts of the object or situation to the functions of the various parts of a bicycle (see ill. 70).

-Explain the comparisons to a group, to a friend, to a sibling or to a parent.

CAN YOU USE THREE INGREDIENTS TO PREPARE A VEGETABLE DISH THAT IS CRUNCHY AND SMOOTH?

THINKING PROCESSES UTILIZED

Critical Thinking:
-classifying ingredients
-ordering problems to form a strategy for planning the recipe

Creative Thinking:
-combining ingredients to create something new
-modifying existing recipes to create something new

Logic:
-recognizing cause and effect relationships
-making predictions based on cause and effect relationships
-designing a strategy for creating a recipe

Problem Solving:
-collecting information to solve a problem

MATERIALS AND EQUIPMENT

Ingredients and Utensils:
This will depend upon the children's suggestions.

Other Preparation:
-experience chart paper or a small sheet of paper depending upon the size of the group
-a duplicated diagram for each child (see ill. 71)

PRE-COOKING ACTIVITIES

ACTIVITY #1 *Define problems.*
Plan a strategy for designing a recipe.

109

Plan a vegetable dish that is crunchy and smooth.

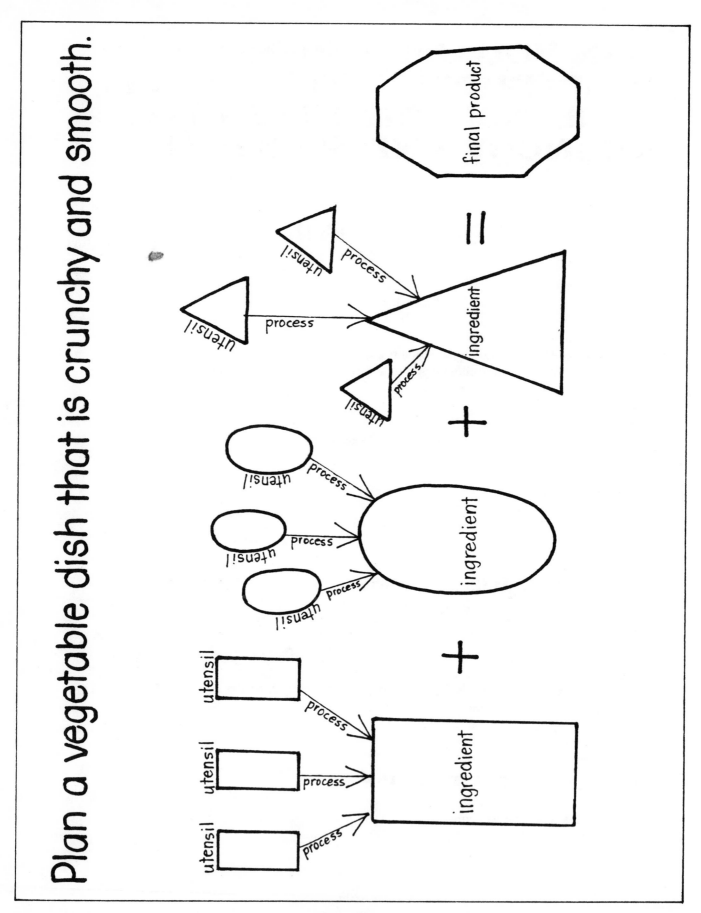

ill. 71

-List the problems you have to consider before you design a recipe for a vegetable dish that is crunchy and smooth.
Record the children's responses.

-Order the problems in a way that presents a logical plan for us to use in designing a recipe.

ACTIVITY #2 *Record the recipe.*

-Consider each of the problems on the above list.
Follow the order you created for solving the problems.
Record your recipe on the diagram.
Encourage children to modify the diagram.

COOKING SUGGESTIONS

You may want to establish further boundaries for the problem by adding different qualifications for the final product. For example: crunchy, smooth and green or crunchy, smooth, green and uncooked.

POST-COOKING ACTIVITIES

ACTIVITY #1 *Practice the skill of solving problems containing specific guidelines.*
(This will depend upon the child's interests and what he/she is studying.)

-How many different ways can you combine three numbers so that the sum is nine and at least two of the addends are even?

-How many words with five or more letters can you think of to describe Peter Pan?

-How many different rhythms can you create that have one quarter rest and three quarter notes?

-What kinds of games can you create if you are on a car trip with two other people, beautiful surrounding scenery, many cars on the road, no books, pencils or paper?

-What kinds of discoveries can you make with a flashlight, a ball and a pencil?

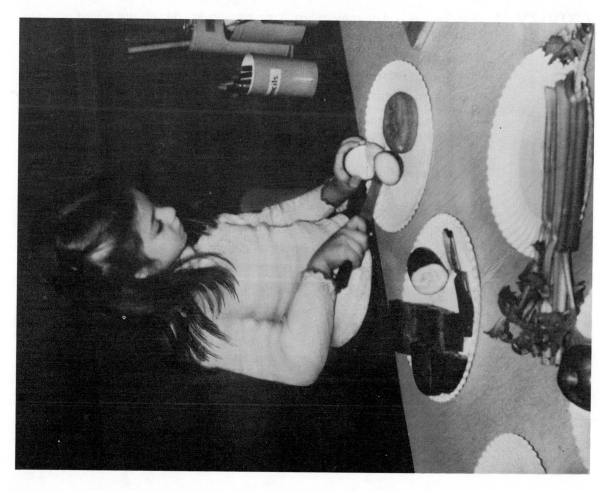

HOW IS A PIECE OF SWISS CHEESE WRAPPED AROUND A FRANKFURTER LIKE A KAZOO?

THINKING PROCESSES UTILIZED

Critical Thinking:
-analyzing objects and ingredients in order to discover their attributes

Creative Thinking:
-substituting different materials and ingredients in order to understand the presence of a variety of concepts in a given situation

Logic:
-using analogies to recognize unapparent relationships

Problem Solving:
-evaluating the final product to see if it meets the necessary criteria

MATERIALS AND EQUIPMENT

Ingredients and Utensils:
-This depends upon the suggestions the children give during the pre-cooking activities.

Other Preparation:
-experience chart paper for a class discussion or a small piece of paper for an individual lesson

PRE-COOKING ACTIVITIES

ACTIVITY #1 *Establish the attributes of Swiss cheese and a kazoo.*
-What are all the different attributes of a piece of Swiss cheese?
-What are all the different attributes of a kazoo?

ACTIVITY #2 *Create an analogy.*
-How is a piece of Swiss cheese wrapped around a frankfurter like a kazoo? (Record children's responses.)

A ballerina dancing with the ballet corps is like a concerto.

Vanessa Age 6

ill. 72

Omar AGE 6

The grass is the orchestra. The tree is the solo.

ill. 73

ACTIVITY #3 *Create a snack that is like a kazoo.*

-How could you prepare a snack that is like a kazoo in at least two ways (see photos)?

COOKING SUGGESTIONS

The children will suggest many different ingredients for the creation of their snack.

If the snack is prepared at school:

-Each child can supply his/her individual ingredients from home.

-An adult can evaluate and purchase a select group of ingredients from a class cooking fund.

POST-COOKING ACTIVITIES

ACTIVITY #1 *Use analogies in other areas to make unfamiliar concepts familiar.*
(This will depend upon what you are studying with the children. The following are a few suggestions.)

-How is a concerto like a particular experience in your environment (see ills. 72 & 73)?

-How is a building like a banana?

-Compare an aspect of your independent study to something else with which you are familiar.

-How is the relationship between music and noise the same as the relationship between a container of milk and spilled milk?
What other relationships can you think of that are similar to music's relationship to noise (see ills. 74 & 75)?

Think of situations in the environment that are
similar to music's relationship to noise.

a smooth road

Greg age 6½   a bumpy road

ill. 74

Think of situations in the environment that are
similar to music's relationship to noise.

a parachute
falling

bricks
falling

Nicole age 7   booM

ill. 75

CAN YOU COMPARE A TUNA FISH SANDWICH WITH A BIRTHDAY AND WRITE A RECIPE THAT COMBINES BOTH SETS OF ATTRIBUTES?

THINKING PROCESSES UTILIZED

Critical Thinking:
-classifying attributes
-regrouping in order to arrive at shared attributes

Creative Thinking:
-combining elements that are apparently unconnected in order to create something new

Logic:
-making analogies in order to stretch the imagination

Problem Solving:
-collecting information in order to gain insight into a problem

MATERIALS AND EQUIPMENT

Ingredients and Utensils:
This will depend upon the children's suggestions.

Other Preparation:
-experience chart paper or a small sheet of paper depending upon the size of the group
-a Venn diagram as shown in ill. 76

PRE-COOKING ACTIVITIES

ACTIVITY #1 *Classify attributes.*
-What are the attributes of a tuna fish sandwich?
-What are the attributes of a birthday?
-Record the children's responses.

117

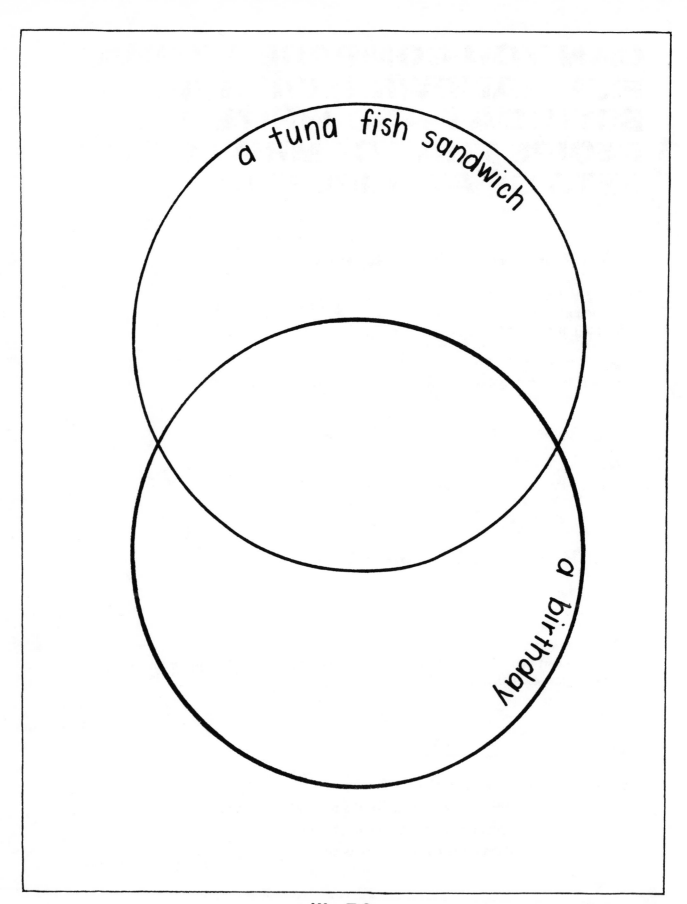

a tuna fish sandwich

a birthday

ill. 76

ACTIVITY #2 *Regroup attributes.*

-Examine both lists of attributes.

Which ones pertain only to a tuna fish sandwich?
Which ones pertain only to a birthday?
Which ones overlap (see ill. 77)?

-Record the children's responses on the Venn diagram.
The intersection will show the attributes that overlap.

ACTIVITY #3 *Make analogies.*

-Use the ideas in the intersection of the Venn diagram to create a Tuna
Birthday Celebration recipe.

-Record a recipe.

COOKING SUGGESTIONS

-A good time to do this is the birthday of a famous person who you are studying or on one of
the children's birthdays.

-If you prepare this lunch in honor of someone you are studying, you can encourage the children
to make a comparison between that person and a birthday instead of a tuna fish sandwich and a
birthday.

POST-COOKING ACTIVITIES

ACTIVITY #1 *Extend the idea of combining apparently dissimilar elements to create
something new.*
The activities will depend upon the child's interests and on what he/she is
studying.

-Draw pictures of sea creatures.
Draw pictures of land animals.
Combine attributes of both to see what early amphibians might have looked
like.

-List the attributes of a table.
List the attributes of a light bulb.
How is a table like a light bulb?
Create a new toy based on the shared attributes of a table and a light bulb.

-How can a musical instrument be proud and angry at the same time?
Create and construct your own musical instrument that can be proud and
angry at the same time.

-List the ingredients and proportions of ingredients you would include in a
hiker's snack (raisins, nuts, chocolates, dried fruits, etc.).

How is a tuna fish sandwich like a birthday?

- There's something fishy about both of them.
- Both are hopes for satisfying hunger.
- Both can leave you in a pickle.
- After a while you'd like to can both of them.
- One is heavy on the mayo. The other is heavy on the ego.
- Both are slices of life.
- Both can be toasted!

Darlene age 21+

ill. 77

How would you package the snack?
How is the training of an athlete like the preparation and packaging of a hiker's snack?

-If a beaver helped a bird build his home, think of all the different ways the home could be designed.

this is   A COOKIE
to CELEBRATE   A
SLEEPOVER PARTY.

A BED

SASCHA.S   age 5½

ill. 78

This cookie is for a
party to
celebrate
winning
Tag.

HANd.

SARAH age 5½

ill. 79

CAN YOU DESIGN A COOKIE THAT WOULD SYMBOLIZE THE LOSS OF A TOOTH?

THINKING PROCESSES UTILIZED

Critical Thinking:
-analyzing an event in order to get the main idea
-classifying symbols to see that symbols can be used in many different situations

Creative Thinking:
-symbolizing an event in order to develop abstract thinking
-brainstorming to develop originality

Logic:
-making deductions about an event in order to create a symbol
-making analogies to gain a better understanding of the concept of a symbol

Problem Solving:
-collecting information about an event in order to create a symbol

MATERIALS AND EQUIPMENT

Ingredients:
-cookie dough
-ingredients suggested by children to decorate their cookies

Utensils:
-This will depend upon the children's suggestions.

Other Preparation:
-writing and/or drawing paper
-crayons, markers and/or pencils
-a duplicated diagram for each child (see ill. 82)
-A recommended book to use with this lesson is, *Symbols and Their Meaning,* by Rolf Myller (New York: Atheneum, 1978).

This cookie is for a party to celebrate catching fish.

fish Alex age 6

ill. 80

This cookie is for a party to celebrate getting a puppy.

Dog

JOSEPH age 5½

ill. 81

My name is _____

ill. 82

My name is *Vanessa G.   age 7* _____

game

piece

a symbol for
myself

a toe shoe

ill. 83

PRE-COOKING ACTIVITIES

ACTIVITY #1 *Recognize symbols in familiar situations.*

-List different kinds of parties you have attended.

-Describe the designs on the cakes or the shapes of the cakes.
Why were those designs and shapes used?

ACTIVITY #2 *Make analogies to understand the meaning of a symbol.*

-How is a traffic light like a heart shaped cake?

-How is a chess piece like a heart shaped cake?
How is it like a traffic light?

-How are a flag, a chess piece, a traffic light and a heart shaped cake the same?

-Introduce and define the word "symbol."

ACTIVITY #3 *Design a cookie to symbolize an event.*

-Think of an unusual event to celebrate with a party.

-Design a cookie that would symbolize the event being celebrated.

-Record the event and the design on a piece of paper.
(See children's work in ill. 78, 79, 80 & 81.)

COOKING SUGGESTIONS

-Encourage children to use their recorded design while preparing their cookies.

-The dough can be prepared in advance so that the child can direct his/her total attention to the creation of his/her originally designed cookie.

POST-COOKING ACTIVITIES

ACTIVITY #1 *Identify different symbols.*
Understand the purpose of using symbols.

-Describe and identify these symbols:
(Select appropriate symbols for the children with whom you work.)

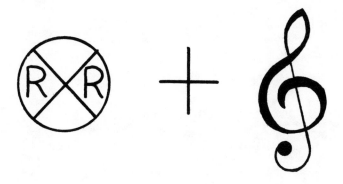

-Why do we use symbols?

ACTIVITY #2 *Each child works with a diagram (see ill. 82).*

-Classify the symbols in each set.

-Add symbols to each set (see ill. 83).

-Draw a symbol or symbols from a category that is not represented on the diagram.

-Draw a symbol to represent yourself.

CAN YOU THINK OF HOW YOU WOULD DECIDE WHICH COLE SLAW RECIPE TO SELECT TO ACCOMPANY TOMORROW'S LUNCH?

THINKING PROCESSES UTILIZED

Critical Thinking:
-comparing and contrasting criteria in order to make a decision

Creative Thinking:
-brainstorming in order to list a multitude of criteria to examine before making a decision

Logic:
-predicting the results of solutions to problems

Problem Solving:
-defining criteria for making a decision

MATERIALS AND EQUIPMENT

Ingredients and Utensils:
This will depend upon the cole slaw recipes you choose (see COOKING SUGGESTIONS).

PRE-COOKING ACTIVITIES

ACTIVITY #1 *Compare two cole slaw recipes.*

   -Read both recipes.

   -How are they the same?

   -How are they different?

ACTIVITY #2 *Select a preferable cole slaw recipe.*

   -What are all the issues you would have to consider before deciding which cole slaw recipe to prepare for tomorrow's lunch?

COOKING SUGGESTIONS

The following are two suggested cole slaw recipes. Each one is for a class of 20 children.

RECIPE I:
-a green shredded cabbage
-⅓ C dark raisins, softened in warm water and drained
-1 medium size apple
-1 ½ C mayonnaise

RECIPE II:
-4 scallions
-1 C mayonnaise
-1 T tomato catsup
-2 t vinegar
-1/8 t Worcestershire Sauce
-¼ t salt
-1/8 t pepper
-¼ t sugar
-3 C shredded cabbage
-3 C salad greens
-1 thinly sliced carrot

POST-COOKING ACTIVITIES

ACTIVITY #1 *Define criteria for helping to make decisions in other situations.*
This will depend upon the child's interests or on what he/she is studying.

-If you are interested in astronomy and in zoology, how can you decide which independent study to do first?

-If you go to a toy store and can only buy one toy, how can you decide which one to buy?

ACTIVITY #2 *Apply decision making strategies to specific curricular areas.*

-Choose the word that best completes the following sentence:
You need_____for a picnic.
        (a basket) (food)

What criteria did you have to consider before selecting the appropriate word?

-Some turtles like to eat chopped meat.
What criteria do you have to consider before preparing a diet for your pet turtle?

-If you could earn $2.00 for preparing dinner or if you could earn $2.00 for babysitting, which job would you choose?
List the criteria you would have to consider in selecting one of the jobs.

-Create similar questions of your own based on the subjects your children are studying or the activities in which they are involved.

Number the processes in their correct order.

____ Place the bread and cheese combination in a broiler or in a toaster oven.

____ Eat the open face sandwich.

____ Take a piece of bread.

____ Watch the bread and cheese combination turn golden brown.

____ Place a slice of cheese on top of the bread.

____ Remove the bread and cheese combination from the heat.

ill. 84

CAN YOU TRANSLATE AN OPEN FACE GRILLED CHEESE SANDWICH RECIPE FOR SOMEONE WHO CANNOT READ OR SPEAK ENGLISH?

THINKING PROCESSES UTILIZED

Critical Thinking:
-analyzing a problem in order to solve it
-ordering processes in order to organize a task

Creative Thinking:
-symbolizing a recipe to transform its original representation

Logic:
-finding a strategy for solving a problem

Problem Solving:
-enumerating problems in a given situation

MATERIALS AND EQUIPMENT

Ingredients:
-bread
-cheese

Utensils:
-a toaster oven or broiler

Other Preparation:
-Record an open face grilled cheese sandwich recipe.
-Record the recipe out of sequence (see ill. 84).

A recipe for an open face grilled cheese sandwich

for someone who cannot read or speak English

CLaUdio age 6

ill. 85

PRE-COOKING ACTIVITIES

ACTIVITY #1 *Order the processes for preparing an open face grilled cheese sandwich.*

-Read the various processes involved in the preparation and completion of the sandwich (see ill. 84).

-Number the processes in their correct order.

ACTIVITY #2 *Translate the recipe.*

-If you had to translate this recipe for someone who did not speak English, what problems would you have to consider?

-What are the different ways you could translate and record the recipe so it could be understood by the non-English speaking person?

-Translate the recipe by drawing symbols (see ill. 85).
Translate the recipe by taking photographs as we cook.
In both cases make sure to include all the processes.

COOKING SUGGESTIONS

Provide an assortment of cheeses so that the children can get used to a variety of tastes. You can also vary the breads.

POST-COOKING ACTIVITIES

ACTIVITY #1 *Symbolize other events.*

-Translate a numerical problem into a number sentence.
For example: Tom and Ruby each bought two pencils.
The pencils cost a nickel apiece.
How much did both pencils cost? 5 + 5 = 10

-Write a rebus story by translating some of the written words into symbols or pictures.

-Translate the symbols on American Indian clothing and ornaments in order to gain a better understanding of various Indian cultures.

-Create your own melody.
Translate the melody into musical notation or ask a friend to do it for you.

-Record a science experiment using symbols only.

-Prepare a symbolic representation of the human body.
Compare the various body parts to aspects of your environment.

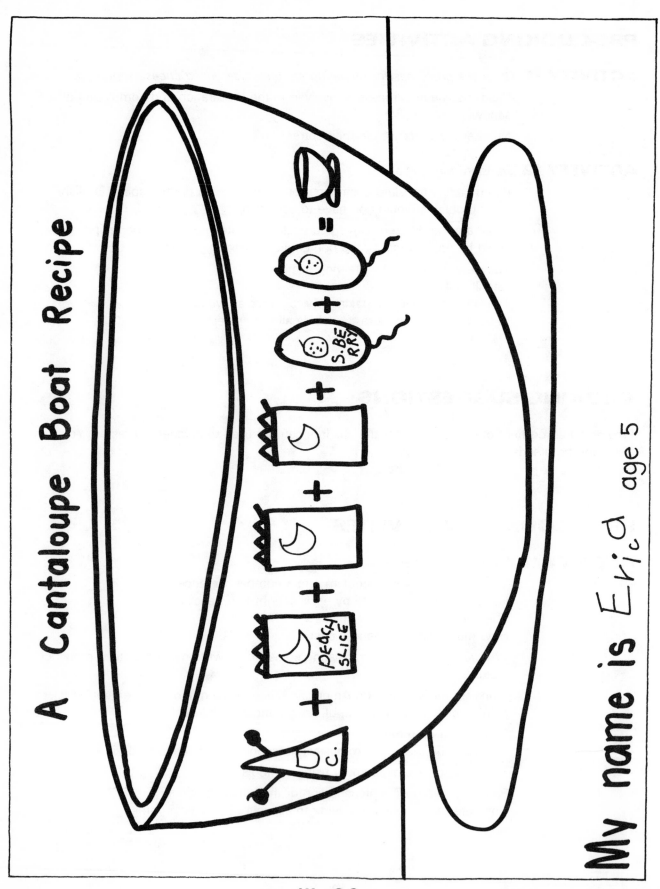

A Cantaloupe Boat Recipe

S. BERRY

PEACH SLICE

My name is Eric age 5

ill. 86

CAN YOU MODIFY AN EXISTING DIAGRAM TO ILLUSTRATE THE INGREDIENTS YOU USED TO MAKE A CANTALOUPE BOAT?

THINKING PROCESSES UTILIZED

Critical Thinking:
-analyzing the relationship of parts to wholes
-translating information into various forms

Creative Thinking:
-modifying an existing item to make it suit your needs
-symbolizing events to record information
-adding ingredients to create something new

Logic:
-patterning in order to create a systematic diagram
-transferring the concept of diagramming to other situations
-making inferences from given information

Problem Solving:
-collecting information and recording it
-evaluating an outcome

MATERIALS AND EQUIPMENT

Ingredients:
-a cantaloupe half or quarter for each child
-ice-cream
-strawberries
-freshly sliced peaches
-sliced bananas

Utensils:
-cutting boards
-knives

-spoons
-ice-cream scoop
-plates

Other Preparation:
-list of ingredients
-a display diagram. The following is a sample:

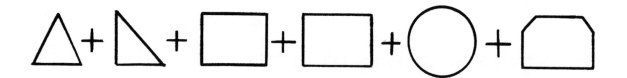

-drawing paper
-pencils

PRE-COOKING ACTIVITIES

ACTIVITY #1 *Plan the dessert.*

    -Examine the list of ingredients.

    -Choose two of the ingredients on the list to fill your cantaloupe boat.

    -How much of each ingredient do you plan to use?

ACTIVITY #2 *Recognize patterns in diagrams.*

    -Examine the display diagram.

    -Create your own rules for recording your desert on this diagram. For example, the same shapes can contain the same ingredients. The shapes can go in the order you add the ingredients.

    -Complete a sample diagram with the children.

ACTIVITY #3 *Modify the class diagram.*

    -Represent the ingredients and the amount you plan to use in a diagram similar to the one we just did together.

    -Modify the diagram to represent accurately your individual recipe (see ill. 86).

COOKING SUGGESTIONS

-A less expensive version of a cantaloupe boat would be a celery stalk boat which can be filled with different ingredients.

-Children should use their diagrams as they prepare their dessert.

POST-COOKING ACTIVITIES

ACTIVITY #1 *Evaluate your recipe.*

-Change your diagram to accommodate any changes you make in your recipe while you prepare it.

ACTIVITY #2 *Use similar diagrams to record other information.*
Establish sets of rules for diagrams.

-You can ask the following kinds of questions based on the rules you establish for similar diagrams:
What does the missing number have to be?

$$\boxed{1} + \boxed{1} + \triangle + \overset{}{\underset{2}{\triangle}} = \langle 6 \rangle$$

What does the missing line have to be?

$$\boxed{1} + \overset{-}{\triangle} + \boxed{} = \langle H \rangle$$

What do the missing letters have to be?

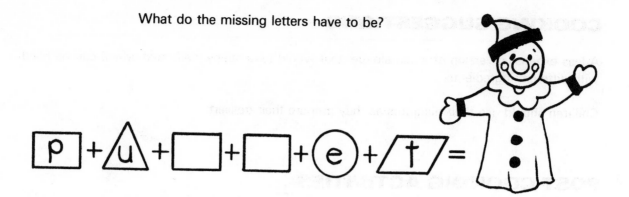

-Experiment with different colors.

-Use a shape diagram to record the colors you can mix to make brown.

-Use a shape diagram to record the tasks you performed in taking care of a plant for three days.

WHAT DO YOU HAVE TO CONSIDER BEFORE YOU PLAN A BANANA DESSERT?

THINKING SKILLS UTILIZED

Critical Thinking:
-analyzing problems in order to plan a strategy
-ordering the ingredients and processes to organize the task

Creative Thinking:
-substituting one ingredient for another
-combining ingredients and performing different processes to create an original product

Logic:
-finding a strategy in order to work more efficiently
-transference of the concept of planning a strategy from cooking to other experiences

Problem Solving:
-gathering information to solve a problem
-defining problems in order to plan a strategy

MATERIALS AND EQUIPMENT

Ingredients and Utensils:
-This will depend upon each child's individually created recipe.

Other Preparation:
-experience chart paper for a large group activity or a small piece of paper for an individual experience.
-duplicated diagrams for each child to prepare his/her banana dessert
(This will depend upon the needs and abilities of the children. See an example of a diagram for six and seven year olds in ill. 87. Older children can create their own plans.)
-individual copies of the Venn diagram seen in ill. 89
-a large diagram for class discussion (see ill. 92)

141

A Banana Dessert Plan

If you don't like bananas, what can you substitute for them?

_____

What ingredients will you use?				
How much of each ingredient will you need?				
Estimate the amount that each will cost.	estimated cost / actual cost	estimated cost / actual cost	estimated cost / actual cost	estimated cost / actual cost
What processes will you use?				
What utensils will you need?				

My name is

ill. 87

A Banana Dessert Plan

If you don't like bananas, what can you substitute for them?

_____

What ingredients will you use?	Banana	cinnamon	graham cracker	chocolate syrup
How much of each ingredient will you need?	2	5 ml	2	25 ml
Estimate the amount that each will cost.	25¢ / 13¢	84¢ / 38¢	99¢ / 1.09	1.00 / 83¢
What processes will you use?	Slice	Sprinkle	Crumble	Pour
What utensils will you need?	Knife			Bowl

My name is Kristin age 6

ill. 88

PRE-COOKING ACTIVITIES

ACTIVITY #1 *Define the problems.*

-If you were going to make a banana dessert, what problems would you have to consider before you got started?

-List them.

ACTIVITY #2 *Design a strategy.*

-Prepare a banana dessert plan.
Before you begin your plan, consider all the problems we listed.

-Younger children can complete an adult prepared diagram based on the problems discussed in ACTIVITY #1.
(See sample of a completed diagram in ill. 88.)

COOKING SUGGESTIONS

-Young children should be encouraged to manipulate measuring utensils in order to make accurate estimates.

-Each child should use his/her recorded plan while preparing this dessert.

POST-COOKING ACTIVITIES

ACTIVITY #1 *Transfer the concept of finding a strategy to other experiences.*
Recognize the use of the same strategies in different experiences.

-In what other situations, besides planning a banana dessert, would you have to use a strategy?
List them.

-Select two different kinds of situations that require the use of a strategy.

-What are the strategies needed in each situation?

-Compare the kinds of strategies used in each one.

-Which strategies are the same for both situations?

ACTIVITY #2 *Use the Venn diagram to record your ideas.*

-Examine the diagram (see ill. 89).

-Select two different kinds of situations that require the use of strategies.

-Complete the diagram so that the shared strategies are recorded in the intersection of the Venn diagram.
(See samples of completed diagrams in ills. 90 & 91.)

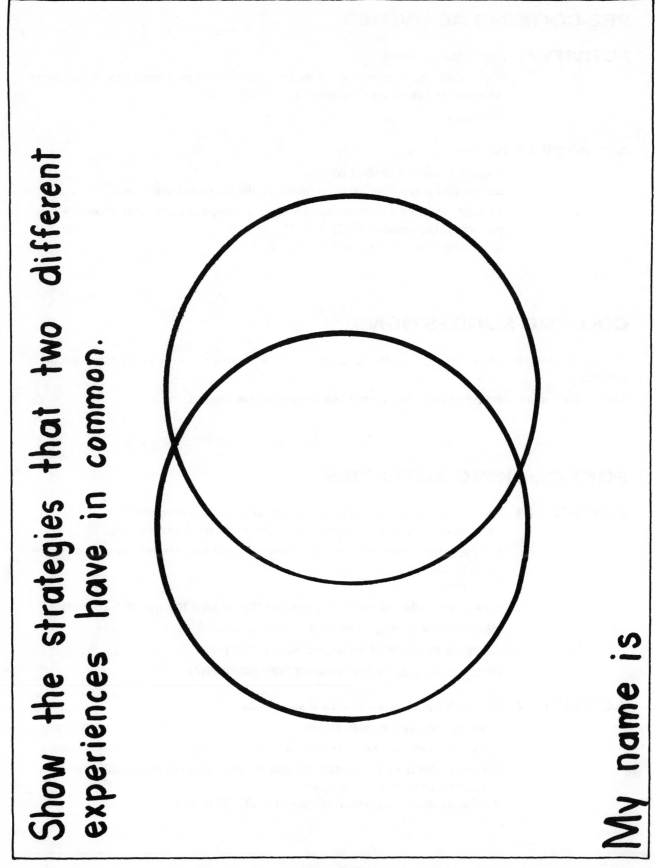

Show the strategies that two different experiences have in common.

My name is

ill. 89

Show the strategies that two different experiences have in common.

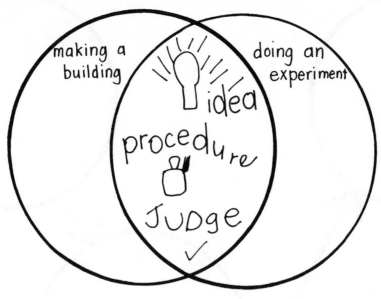

making a building

doing an experiment

idea
procedure
JUDGe ✓

My name is zachary. age 6

ill. 90

Show the strategies that two different experiences have in common.

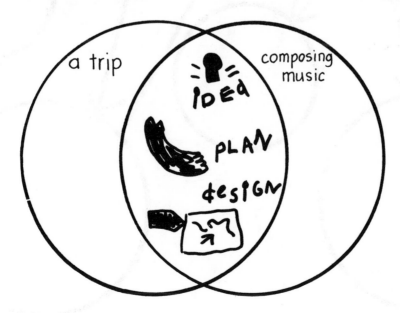

a trip

composing music

IDEa
PLAN
desfGN

My name is JOSEPH. age 5½

ill. 91

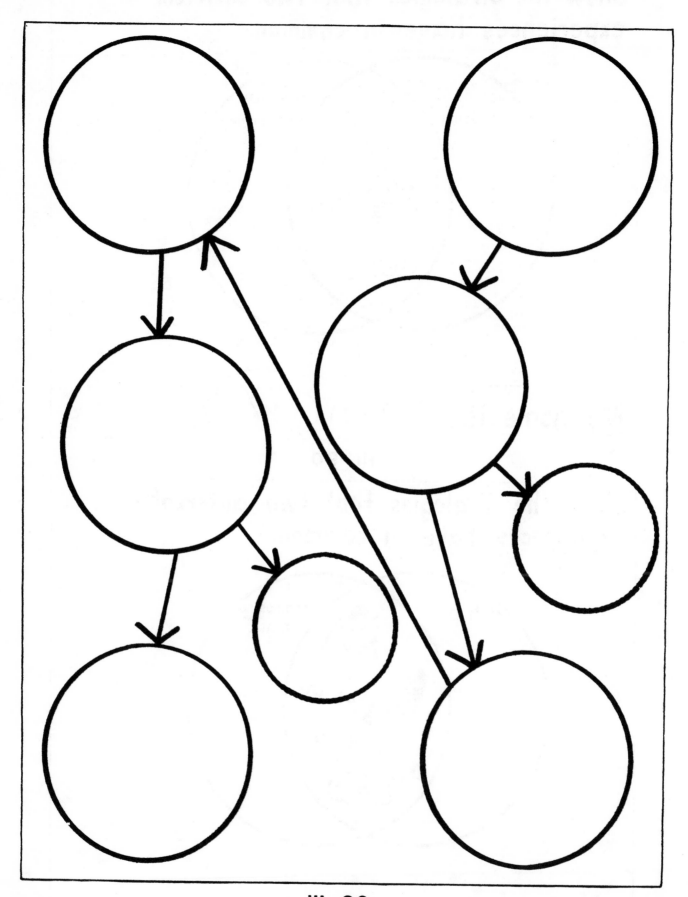

ill. 92

ACTIVITY #3 *Plan a strategy for a real problem.*

(The following is a sample lesson.)

-What if a blizzard began while you were at school?

-What problems would you face?

-What strategies would you use?

-Plan a strategy for one of the problems.

-Use the diagram in ill. 92 to plan your strategy.

-If necessary, make additions to the diagram or create your own diagram.
(This activity can be done as a group or individually.)

ACTIVITY #4 *Define problems in specific curricular areas.*
Design a strategy to solve each problem.

-What different strategies could you use to decode a word you can't read?

-Examine a numerical equation with an unknown:

$$7 = X + 5$$

What is the problem?
How can you solve it?

-What problems are involved in inviting some of the children at school to watch you dance at your afterschool ballet class?
Plan a strategy for solving the problems.

-What strategies can you use to build a block structure that is taller than you?

-What strategies would be most effective in assembling a 500 piece puzzle?

-Ask similar kinds of questions in other areas in which the children are involved.

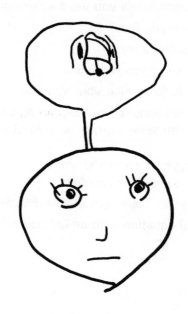

ill. 93

ill. 94

HOW MANY WAYS CAN YOU USE YOUR BEAN?

THINKING PROCESSES UTILIZED

Critical Thinking:
-analyzing the attributes of specific foods in order to create analogies
-comparing attributes of various foods to situations in our environment with similar attributes

Creative Thinking:
-substituting words to change the meaning of a sentence
-symbolizing an event by representing it with a kind of food
-symbolizing an event with a figure of speech

Logic:
-recognizing the effect of the use of a specific food in a figure of speech

Problem Solving:
-gathering information to gain a better understanding of a situation
-hypothesizing about the origin of particular figures of speech
-justifying the use of particular foods used in various figures of speech

MATERIALS AND EQUIPMENT

Ingredients and Utensils:
This will depend upon the children's suggestions.

Other preparation:
-Experience chart paper or a small sheet of paper, depending upon the size of the group
-sample foods used in PRE-COOKING ACTIVITY #3
-cookbooks
-a book of colloquialisms, slang, or daily expressions

PRE-COOKING ACTIVITIES

ACTIVITY #1 *Analyze foods to help decode figures of speech.*
-Exhibit some of the foods included in the figures of speech in ACTIVITY #3.
-Describe the attributes of corn, onions, grapes, etc.

149

-Record the children's responses.

ACTIVITY #2 *Compare the attributes of the various foods in ACTIVITY #1 with experiences in our environment.*

-Use the attributes listed for each food used in ACTIVITY #1 to cite an analagous situation in our environment. For example, the pattern of kernels on an ear of corn is like a repetitive piece of music.

ACTIVITY #3 *Analyze colloquialisms that include food.*
Compare various figures of speech.
Define "Figures of Speech."

-Read the following pairs of sentences.
How are they the same?

-That toy isn't worth a hill of beans.
That toy has no value.

-That's a plum of an idea.
That's a very good idea.

-You're full of bologna.
You're not telling the truth.

-That's corny.
That's not very clever.

-He knows his onions.
He knows what he's doing.

-Can you cut the mustard?
Can you do it?

-That's peachy!
That's fine!

-Don't spill the beans!
Don't tell anyone else!

-Something's fishy!
I don't trust what's going on!

-Beef up the story you wrote.
Make your story more interesting.

-Don't be chicken.
Don't be a coward.

-That's a fine kettle of fish!
That's not a good situation!

-He's a car nut.
He's really involved with cars.

-She has a finger in every pie.
She's involved in many different things.

-She's the apple of his eye.
She's the girl he likes best.

-He's a good egg.
 He's a good fellow.

-She has sour grapes because she didn't get invited to the party.
 She is ill-tempered because she didn't get invited to the party.

-Introduce and define the concept, "figure of speech".

ACTIVITY #4 *Hypothesize about the origin of each of the expressions.*

-Justify the use of the particular food mentioned in each figure of speech.

-Substitute other foods for the ones mentioned.
 How does it change the expression?

-If possible, supply the children with the actual derivation of each expression.

ACTIVITY #5 *Prepare a recipe that illustrates the meaning of one of the figures of speech.*

-Select one of the figures of speech to serve as the name of a recipe.

-Use a cookbook to help you select a recipe that has the same attributes as a particular figure of speech.
 You can create your own recipe instead of using a pre-written one. Here are some ideas:

-That's peachy (That's fine!)
 Recipe: Peach Melba

-Something's fishy! (I don't trust what's going on!)
 Recipe: Baked fish with a surprise stuffing

-Don't spill the beans! (Don't tell anyone else!)
 Recipe: Vegetable soup with only one bean

COOKING SUGGESTIONS

-The recipes can be accumulated or developed as a group activity or as an independent activity.

-A lunch or dinner can be developed around the idea expressed in a figure of speech. Three different recipes can be selected to create the menu.

-If you are working with an entire class, the group can select and prepare one of the recipes, or they can be divided into small groups to prepare many different recipes. Another option is to have the children prepare the recipes at home.

POST-COOKING ACTIVITIES

ACTIVITY #1 *Compare yourself to a food.*

-Choose a fruit or a vegetable.

-List all its qualities.

-What are the different ways you are like that fruit or vegetable?

ACTIVITY #2 *Draw a symbol to represent a figure of speech.*

-Take a survey of common figures of speech.
Ask friends, family and/or look in special reference books that include figures of speech.

-Draw a symbol to represent a figure of speech (see ills. 93 & 94).

-Ask a friend to guess the expression.

ACTIVITY #3 *Match different expressions with various professions.*
Create figures of speech.

-Record different kinds of jobs.

-What figures of speech can we associate with a particular occupation?
Use existing colloquialisms or create your own.

-Some samples follow:

An electrician might say: "Charlie has magnetism."

A chemist might say: "There's a chemistry between Wendy and Steve."

A ski instructor might say: "It's all downhill from here."

A grocer might say: "It's in the bag!"

A pilot might say: "I'm up in the air about what I should do."

A bus driver might say: "That rings a bell."

An ophthalmologist might say: "Let's see eye to eye!"

-For very young children the above activity can be done as a matching exercise.
The children can match the saying with the occupation.

ACTIVITY #4 *Create an original figure of speech by substituting words.*

-Substitute a word or words in a particular figure of speech.
How does the meaning change?

-The following are a few examples:

If "Lend me an ear," means "Listen to me," how could you say, "Look at me?"

If "I'm down in the dumps," means "I'm feeling sad," how could you say, "I'm feeling happy?"

If "Let's wrap it up," means "Let's finish it," how could you say, "Let's start it?"

CAN YOU CREATE AND EVALUATE YOUR OWN MIXED DRINK?

THINKING PROCESSES UTILIZED

Critical Thinking:
-analyzing information to create a name for the drink and to evaluate a drink

Creative Thinking:
-combining elements to create something new
-transforming a recipe into diagram form

Logic:
-predicting the effects of adding certain ingredients

Problem Solving:
-collecting information to create a recipe
-evaluating ingredients and processes
-justifying the combination of ingredients and the processes used
-collecting information to define a problem

MATERIALS AND EQUIPMENT

Ingredients and Utensils:
-These will depend upon the children's suggestions.

Other Preparation:
-duplicated diagrams of ill. 96 for each child
-unlined paper
-pencils
-experience chart paper or a small piece of paper depending upon the size of the group

PRE-COOKING ACTIVITIES

ACTIVITY #1 *Collect information to help create the drink.*
-List different ingredients that you could include in a mixed drink.

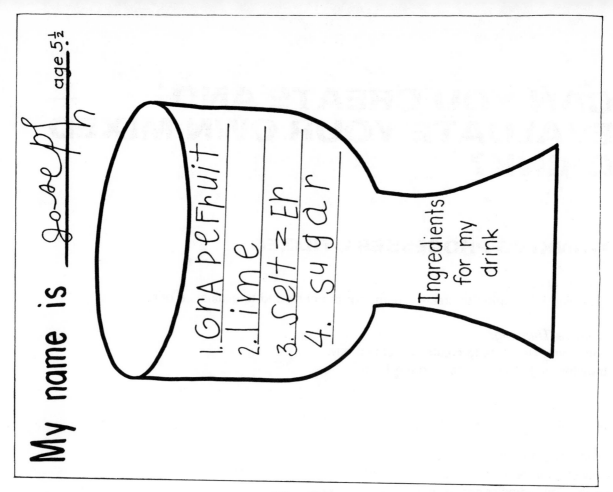

My name is _Joseph_ age 5½

1. Grapefruit
2. lime
3. seltzer
4. sugar

Ingredients for my drink

ill. 95

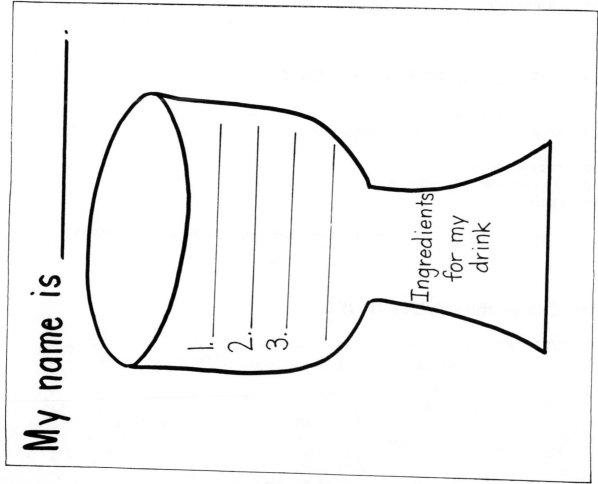

My name is _____

1. _____
2. _____
3. _____

Ingredients for my drink

ill. 96

ACTIVITY #2   *Define the drink.*
Evaluate the idea.

-Create your own drink using three or four ingredients from the above list.

-Why did you select those ingredients?

-Record the ingredients on the duplicated diagram (see ill. 95).

-Exchange diagrams with a friend to hear his/her suggestions.

ACTIVITY #3   *Evaluate the diagram in ACTIVITY #2.*

-Examine a completed ingredients diagram.

-If another person wanted to prepare your drink, what problems would he/she have with your diagram?

-How could you make the diagram more complete?

-How would you have to change the existing diagram?

ACTIVITY #4   *Create a diagram.*

-Design a diagram that would show a friend exactly how to prepare your drink.

-Consider the issues we discussed before you create your diagram (see ills. 97 & 98).

ACTIVITY #5   *Create a name for the drink.*

-Think of different names for your drink.

-Pick the best one.

-Why did you choose that one?

COOKING SUGGESTIONS:

Children should follow their individual diagrams in the preparation of their drinks. This will give them an opportunity to evaluate the effectiveness of their diagrams and to see how their diagrams might be improved.

POST-COOKING ACTIVITIES

ACTIVITY #1   *Evaluate the drink.*

-List criteria for evaluating your mixed drink.
(Record children's responses.)

ingredients quantity process order

utensils: tablespoon and cup

1 lemon juice — pour

2 whipped cream — Put — 3/4 cup

lime juice — squeeze — whole — 1/4 cup

3 blend everything

Titli age 6½

ill. 97

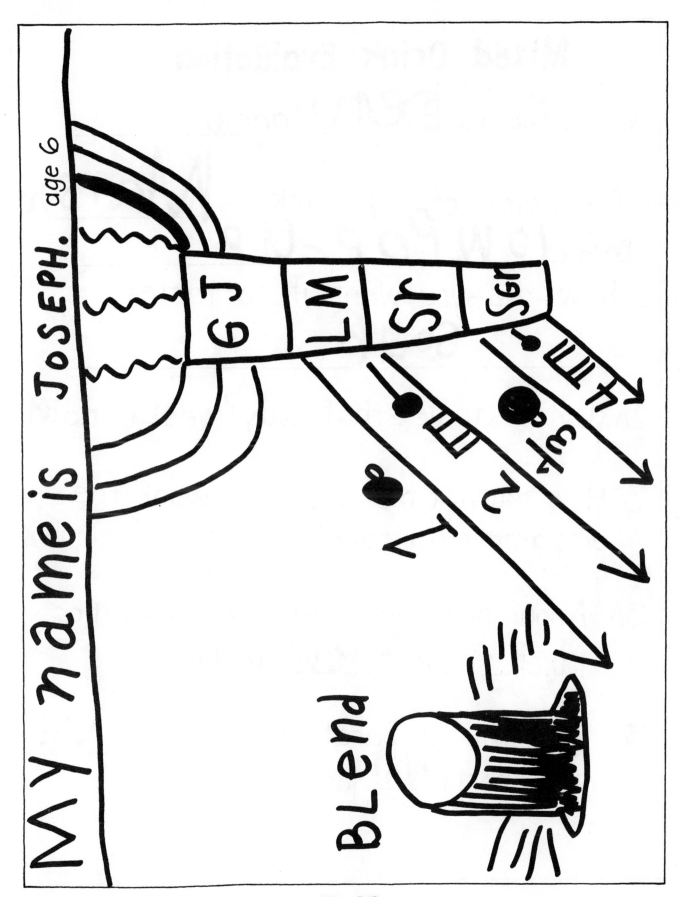

ill. 98

Mixed Drink Evaluation

My name is __Ben__ age 6 _____.

1. The name of my drink is __Marsh-__
__mallow Pop-up_____.

2. How did you want it to taste?
__Sour_____

2A. Did it taste that way? yes ☐ no ☑

3. How much time did you want the preparation to take? ____ hours _1_ minutes

3A. About how long did the preparation take? __ hours __a few__ minutes

3B. Was the preparation too long? __NO!__ too short? __No!__ just right? __yes__

Mixed Drink Evaluation

4. Did you have all the ingredients you needed? yes ☑ no ☐

5. Did your procedure work? yes ☐ no ☑

6. Did you plan too much of any ingredient? yes ☑ no ☐
Which one? _Soda sugar_

6A. Did you plan too little of any ingredient?
yes ☑ no ☐
Which one? _lime_

7. Did you change your drink? yes ☑ no ☐

subtract	add
Sugar	lime

8. How would you rate your drink?
good

ill. 100

What else can you evaluate?

a birthday party (Caroline)

a painting (Vanessa)

an experience at an ice cream store (Ben)

a group of activities (Sascha)

the quality of a store (Kyla)

a piece of clothing (Alex)

work (David)

how well you play an instrument (Joseph)

the price of something (Kristin)

a show (Raymond)

sound (Omar)

amount of light (Titli)

what you say (Philip)

a toy (Sarah)

food (Emmaia)

ill. 101

ACTIVITY #2 *Complete an evaluation form.*

-An adult can prepare a set of evaluation forms based on the children's responses. The children complete the forms. Older children can prepare their own forms (see ills. 99 & 100).

ACTIVITY #3 *Extend the idea of evaluation to other situations.*

-What else can you evaluate?

-List all your ideas and explain them (see ill. 101).

NOTES